I0446767

You're about to learn the secrets to saving at least $7,000 in taxes, without hiring an expensive CPA or attorney to do it for you!

Legal Disclaimers:

This system was designed to be implemented for your service business as a sole proprietor (single owner) being paid on a 1099 contractor basis. This might include real estate agents, musicians, graphic designers, petroleum landmen, artists, independent salespeople, etc. This system is not designed for any other business that involves owning significant assets, such as real estate or financial investments, equipment, or inventory, as there are specific legal and tax planning strategies that pertain to those types of businesses that this system doesn't cover. The information provided in this ebook is not legal advice, but general information on legal and tax issues commonly encountered while working with specific clients. We are not a CPA or law firm and the information included herein should not be construed as a substitute for seeking the advice of an attorney or tax professional to make sure this is a strategy that makes sense for your particular circumstances.

TABLE OF CONTENTS

Introduction 4

System Overview 5

Step 1: Setting Up Your LLC 9

Step 2: File Other Critical Forms with the IRS 28

Step 3: Open Bank Account 46

Step 4: Pay Yourself a Salary.. 48

Step 5: Lease Your Vehicle to Your LLC 63

Step 6: Reimburse for Home Office Expenses 64

Step 7: Set Aside Money to Pay Taxes 66

Step 8: Pay Yourself a Tax-Free Dividend 67

Step 9: Plan Your Next Vacation 68

Bonus Tip: Avoid the Underpayment Penalty 69

Recap of Filing Requirements 71

Final Words 73

Appendix A – Quick & Easy Cash Flow Plan 74

Appendix B – Tax Savings 5-Year Projection 75

Appendix C – Automobile Lease 76

Appendix D – LLC Operating Agreement 79

Introduction

This ebook was written with a single goal in mind, to help you beat the IRS at their own game!

I know from my experience helping hundreds of other "solopreneurs" like yourself that you're going to start reaping some huge tax benefits by implementing the simple steps outlined here.

So, you're probably asking yourself, "who is this guy that I should even consider following any of these strategies?" Hi, my name is Liam Robinson and for nearly 20 years I worked as a tax advisor to small business owners in the Houston area. During that time I prepared well over 1,500 personal and business tax returns and set up hundreds of new entities (LLC, S-Corp, partnership, etc.) for self-employed clients.

Over the course of working with these clients, I started to realize that most of them were never quite 100% sure how to handle their taxes, since there's not exactly a mandatory course in your training to become an entrepreneur. So what I found was that nearly 85% of them were paying way too much in taxes, either because they weren't properly advised when they first started their business, or they thought it would be too complicated for them to maintain a separate legal entity.

So I decided to write this ebook for YOU! These concepts apply to just about anyone working as a sole proprietor, so whether you're an independent salesperson, actor, YouTube celebrity, solo architect, network marketing guru, personal coach, or real estate agent, this system can work for you. When you follow this sytem to properly set up your own LLC, you'll be able to put thousands of tax dollars back in your pocket, protect your hard-earned assets against lawsuits, and substantially reduce your risk of an IRS audit.

In the following pages, I'll be walking you through some fairly simple, yet extremely powerful and effective tax strategies that have been tested and refined over many years with fantastic results. So what I've done is put these strategies together in an easy-to-follow, "do-it-yourself" format, tailored specifically for you as a solopreneur. And whether you actually follow this system and set up your LLC by yourself, or take what you've learned and have a more informed discussion with your CPA on your specific tax situation, you are guaranteed to save hundreds of thousands of tax dollars over the course of your career.

So let's stop wasting time and get right down to business!

System Overview

Here's a bird's eye view of what we'll be covering in the following pages of The Freelancer's LLC Playbook. If you follow this system to the "T", I guarantee you can reap some serious tax savings come next tax season. This is the basic blueprint, and we'll be delving into each of these in more detail over the next few sections.

1. Set up your LLC (Don't worry, it's a lot easier than you think.)

2. Obtain an EIN, plus the most important form you'll file for your new LLC

3. Open a business bank account

4. Pay yourself a "reasonable" salary

5. Pay yourself a "reasonable" lease for the business use of your vehicle

6. Reimburse yourself for home office expenses

7. Set aside money to pay your taxes

8. Pay yourself a tax-free dividend

9. Plan your next vacation (you deserve it!)

10. Bonus tip: how to pay yourself once to avoid the IRS underpayment penalty

But before we get into the nuts and bolts of this system, let's make sure you understand the benefits of having an LLC in the first place.

Benefits of an LLC

Establishing an LLC (or any type of corporation or partnership for that matter) can provide you with 3 main benefits if set up correctly: liability protection, tax savings, and minimizing audit risk.

Liability protection simply means that if there's ever a lawsuit that arises from your business, the LLC acts as a shield to protect your personal assets (anything that is held in your personal name and not in the name of the business). For instance, if you have a retirement account that's in your personal name, and someone sues your real estate business for whatever reason, they can only come after the assets of the business (which in this particular setup, is practically nothing but whatever cash you hold in your business bank account). Now there typically isn't much of an issue with a freelancer being sued, and if they are, an Errors & Omissions or Umbrella Insurance policy would typically cover any damages. But the LLC structure does offer another layer of protection, just to be safe.

There is a plethora of tax advantages, depending on your particular situation. The main tax advantage is that it allows you to control how much of your income is subject to that nasty 15% self-employment tax (which remember is on top of your normal "marginal" tax rate), but an LLC also allows you to write off even more expenses by setting up a medical reimbursement plan, set aside more pre-tax money into a retirement account, deduct your children's college expenses (if you hire your children for a little while), take a portion of your household expenses as a home office deduction, and so much more.

Operating your business through an LLC also significantly reduces your risk of being audited by the IRS, because it prevents you from having to file a Schedule C with your personal tax return, which is the equivalent of putting an elephant-sized target on your bank account for the IRS during open hunting season! I mean, at that point you might as well just take ¼ of all your hard-earned dollars and throw a huge "IRS agents only" block party to celebrate all those well-deserving tax fiduciaries.

According to the IRS Data Book that's published every year, between all the Schedule C, Corporations, Partnerships, and LLCs, over 38 million business-related tax returns were filed in 2019, and out of those, only 3,186 LLC/S-Corp returns were audited compared to over 444,000 Schedule C audits. Knowing that little tidbit of information, my question to you now is why would you want to continue filing a Schedule C for even one more year, if you're over 100 times more likely to be audited than someone operating through an LLC or S-Corp?!

BUSINESSES AUDITED BY THE IRS IN 2019

Schedule C	444,800
LLC/S-Corp	3,186

Now that you hopefully understand the massive benefits of operating through an LLC, let's take a quick look at a scenario that is pretty typical of someone making an average living as a freelancer, and what her taxes would look like if she didn't follow our system.

REAL-LIFE (SORT OF) EXAMPLE:
(We did change the names to protect her good reputation)

Ima Goodshot is a 27-year-old single woman who has been working for the past 18 months as an independent photographer. Her average monthly sales are $8,000 and out-of-pocket business expenses average $1,800/month, leaving her with around $6,200/month net. This comes out to $74,400 per year of taxable income.

Since Ima doesn't yet know about "The Freelancer's LLC Method", she files her tax return on April 15th and ends up having to shell out over $18,000 in taxes.

Well, what she didn't realize was that on top of her regular income tax rate for individuals, she's considered self-employed, so a good chunk of that $18,000 is herself-employment tax, which takes an additional 15.3% of her $74,400 income.

A better alternative for Ima would be to follow our system by setting up an LLC and paying herself a small "reasonable" salary out of the LLC, let's say $18,000 a year just to start out, so that only her $18,000 salary is subject to the additional 15.3% tax, instead of the entire $74,400. In this scenario, her total tax would only be around $10,000, which is a tax savings of over $8,000 in the first year alone!

Now I'm sure you're saying, "Yeah, but how much does it cost to set up and maintain an LLC?" It's actually a lot less than you might think. We're going to cover all that in a few minutes, but just to give you an idea, if you do everything yourself according to the following instructions, you can expect to spend around anywhere from $300-$500 (depending on your state's filing fee) upfront to get it all set up and then less than $1,000 per year thereafter to maintain it. That's a pretty good investment for a return of $8,000 in tax savings each year.

Realistically, as your income increases to the 6-figure range, you should experience tax savings more in the neighborhood of $13k-15k per year. Just think about how much that will add up to over the course of your career and how many luxury vacations you could afford!

If you want to get a better idea of how much you can save using this system, take a look at the "Freelancer's Tax Savings Projection" spreadsheet in the Appendix, which gives a 5-year projection of tax savings. You may even be inclined to slap yo mama after realizing how much you could save using this method!

Alright, now that we've established the fact that you're definitely going to be saving some serious cash with this system, let's go ahead and get into the nuts and bolts of how to get your business set up and running like a well-oiled, tax-saving machine.

Step 1:
Create Your LLC and DBA

A quick Google search for "Setup an LLC" will yield hundreds, if not thousands of results for businesses that offer this service, the most popular of which are probably LegalZoom and ZenBusiness, but in all my years of experience, I've found it just as easy, and cheaper, to go directly through the Secretary of State's (SOS) website (as long as you know what you're doing). Assuming the reason you bought this DIY book in the first place was to save a little money, by going through the SOS site directly, you're only going to pay the required state filing fee and not an additional $100-300 to a third party to do the same thing I'm about to teach you how to do yourself.

Also, if you were to go through any of these third-party online services, they're going to hit you with 1,000 annoying up-sells during the process, everything from merchant services and banking to compliance protection and diaper changing services (not really that last one, but it definitely seems like they throw every one of their affiliate promotions at you before submitting your filing!) PLUS, they're primarily focused on the legal entity structure, and not so much on the tax benefits, so it's critical to answer the questions according to my recommendations below to ensure maximum tax benefits, and that you don't pay for any unnecessary services.

By the way, you'll notice that I'll be walking through the questionnaire on the Texas SOS website (sorry, I don't have the time or patience to walk through this for all 50 states, but for the most part they're pretty similar as far as the questions they'll be asking), so all you have to do is answer them as indicated and you'll be on your way to having your own real, live LLC (kinda like Pinocchio but without that annoying sidekick of his). And feel free to call me "Captain Obvious", but I should point out that you'll want to input your own personal information in each of the fields and not mine that's indicated on the screenshots. Duh😬

Ok, so go ahead and click your state on the next page to get started.

- **Alabama**: https://www.alabamainteractive.org/sos/introduction_input.action
- **Alaska**: https://www.commerce.alaska.gov/web/cbpl/Corporations/OnlineFilingInstructionsLLCArticles.aspx
- **Arizona**: https://ecorp.azcc.gov
- **Arkansas**: https://www.ark.org/sos/corpfilings/index.php
- **California**: https://idm.sos.ca.gov
- **Colorado**: https://www.sos.state.co.us/pubs/business/helpFiles/LLCintro.html
- **Connecticut**: https://service.ct.gov/business
- **Delaware**: https://corp.delaware.gov/howtoform/
- **Florida**: https://dos.myflorida.com/sunbiz/start-business/efile/fl-llc/
- **Georgia**: https://georgia.gov/register-llc
- **Hawaii**: https://cca.hawaii.gov/breg/registration/dllc/
- **Idaho**: https://sosbiz.idaho.gov/
- **Illinois**: https://www.ilsos.gov/departments/business_services/organization/llc_instructions.html
- **Indiana**: https://inbiz.in.gov/BOS/Home/Index
- **Iowa**: https://filings.sos.iowa.gov/Account/Login
- **Kansas**: https://www.kansas.gov/
- **Kentucky**: https://web.sos.ky.gov/fasttrack/
- **Louisiana**: https://geauxbiz.sos.la.gov
- **Maine**: https://www.maine.gov/sos/cec/corp/incorporating.html
- **Maryland**: https://egov.maryland.gov/businessexpress
- **Massachusetts**: https://www.sec.state.ma.us/cor/corpweb/corllc/llcinf.htm
- **Michigan**: https://cofs.lara.state.mi.us/corpweb/LoginSystem/ExternalLogin.aspx
- **Minnesota**: https://www.sos.state.mn.us/business-liens/start-a-business/how-to-register-your-business/
- **Mississippi**: https://corp.sos.ms.gov/corp/portal/c/page/login/portal.aspx
- **Missouri**: https://www.sos.mo.gov/business/corporations/startbusiness#entityReg
- **Montana**: https://sosmt.gov/business/how-do-i/
- **Nebraska**: https://sos.nebraska.gov/business-services/forms-and-fee-information
- **Nevada**: https://www.nvsilverflume.gov/startBusiness
- **New Hampshire**: https://quickstart.sos.nh.gov/online/Account/LoginPage?LoginType=CreateNewBusiness
- **New Jersey**: https://www.njportal.com/dor/businessformation/home/welcome
- **New Mexico**: https://portal.sos.state.nm.us/BFS/online/Account
- **New York**: https://www.businessexpress.ny.gov/app/answers/cms/a_id/2443/kw/domestic%20LLC
- **North Carolina**: https://www.sosnc.gov/Online_Services/
- **North Dakota**: https://firststop.sos.nd.gov/forms/new/523
- **Ohio**: https://bsportal.ohiosos.gov/Login.aspx
- **Oklahoma**: https://www.sos.ok.gov/
- **Oregon**: https://secure.sos.state.or.us/
- **Pennsylvania**: https://www.corporations.pa.gov
- **Rhode Island**: https://www.sos.ri.gov/divisions/business-services/ri-business/start-your-rhode-island-business
- **South Carolina**: https://businessfilings.sc.gov/businessfiling
- **South Dakota**: https://sosenterprise.sd.gov/BusinessServices/Business/RegistrationInstr.aspx
- **Tennessee**: https://tnbear.tn.gov/Ecommerce/RegistrationInstr.aspx
- **Texas**: https://direct.sos.state.tx.us/acct/acct-login.asp
- **Utah**: https://secure.utah.gov/
- **Vermont**: https://bizfilings.vermont.gov/online/Home/
- **Virginia**: https://cis.scc.virginia.gov
- **Washington**: https://ccfs.sos.wa.gov#/
- **West Virginia**: https://onestop.wv.gov/b4wvpublic/default.aspx
- **Wisconsin**: https://onestop.wi.gov/OpenMyBusiness
- **Wyoming**: https://wyobiz.wyo.gov/Business/RegistrationInstr.aspx

Most states will require you to first register for an online account before you can request your LLC, so do that first, then look for a link that says something about filing online for a "Domestic Limited Liability Company" (domestic just means you have a business presence in the state where you're filing, whereas foreign is used when a business outside of your state wants to create a presence there), or sometimes it will say "File Articles of Organization", and then meet me back here.

For Texas SOS account setup:

Click the Texas link on the prior page, then the "request for SOSDirect Account" link.

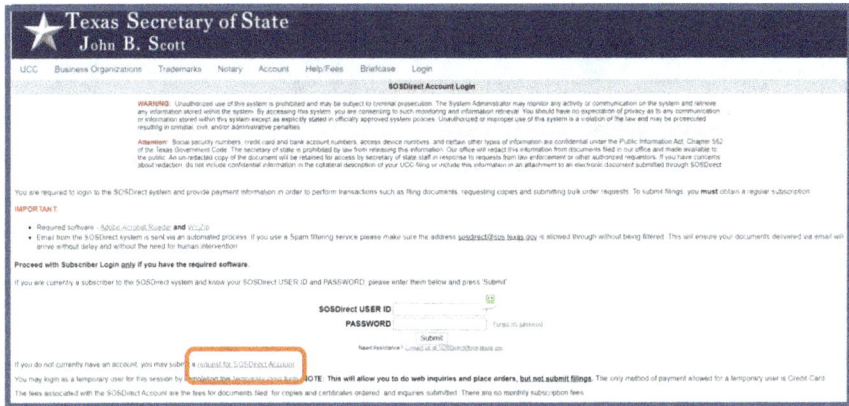

On the next screen, enter your name, not a business name. The business name field is just if you were paying a third-party business to set this up for you, so leave it blank.

Now that you've set up your online account and logged in, the next two screens will ask for your payment method and contact info. Select "credit card" as your payment method (even if you're using a debit card).

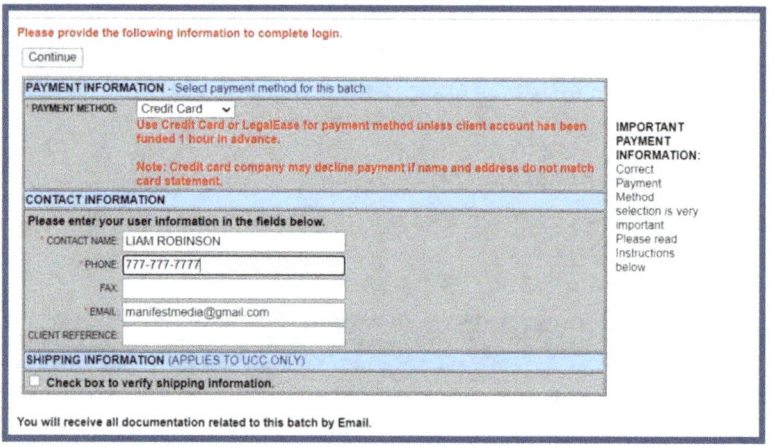

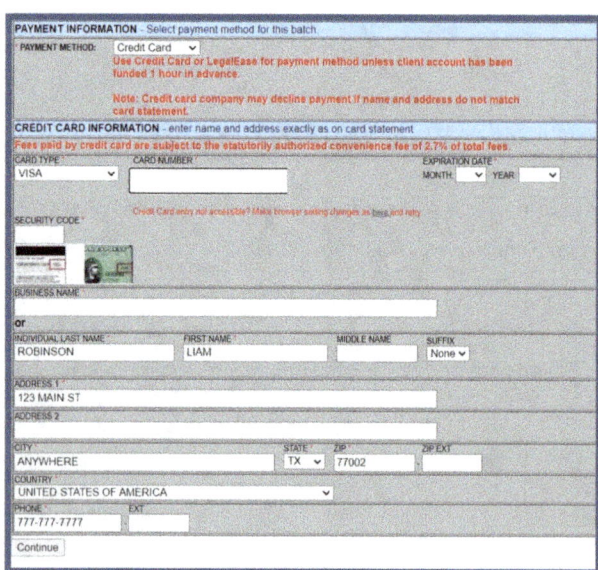

After you enter all of your information and click the "Continue" button at the bottom, it will take you to the next screen saying that you're logged in. At the top of that screen, you'll want to select "Business Organizations" on the top menu.

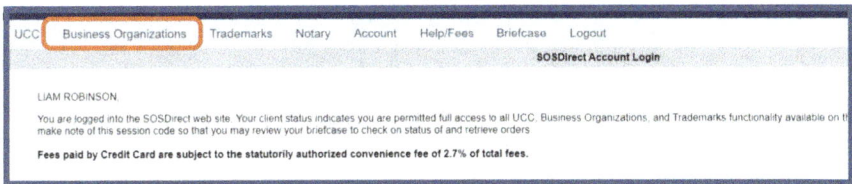

You should be viewing the Business Organizations Menu screen now, where you'll select "Domestic Limited Liability Company" from the drop-down menu, then click the "File Document" button next to it.

BUSINESS ORGANIZATIONS MENU

CLIENT REFERENCE (optional): [NONE]

● Client Reference:	Update Client Reference

INQUIRIES AND ORDERS

● Name Availability Search	● Filing Number Search
● Find - Entity	● FEIN Search
● Find - Supplemental	● TID Search
● Find - Global	● Document Number Search
● Find - Assumed Name	● Order - Certificates and Copies
● Find - People	● Bulk Order - Data
● Find - Registered Agent	● Registered Agent activity past 60 days

WEB FILINGS

DO NOT USE 'BACK' BUTTON
Use of the 'BACK' button during the "WEB FILINGS" process will result
in loss of data. Please press the 'Cancel Filing' button and start again.

● Reservation * Formation * Registration Documents
First select the type of entity for which you wish to submit a filing, and then click 'File Document'

Domestic Limited Liability Company (LLC) ⌄   File Document

File assumed name certificates, changes to registered office/agent, dissolutions, reinstatements, cancellations, withdrawals and annual statements as change documents.

● Change Documents
Enter filing number and click 'File Document' or click 'Find Entity'

[   ]   Find Entity   File Document

● Master Filing

● Master Filing Search/Cost Estimator

On this screen, select "Certificate of Formation" from the drop-down (the only option).

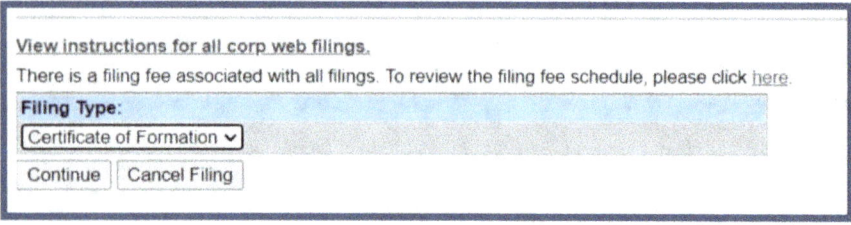

Next, select Limited Liability Company as the Organization Type and enter the name you want for your LLC, including "LLC" at the end of the name, then click the "Name Availability Search" button. You'll need to pick a unique name that's not already taken by someone else in your state, so you might try your name, followed by "Consulting Services" or something like that. Usually a name availability search only costs $1 (if anything) and will ensure that your filing doesn't get kicked back because someone else's business name is too similar. The name availability search will return results with the most similar names that are already taken, in case you need to tweak yours a bit. I wouldn't spend too much time overthinking the name here, because I'm also going to show you next how to create a DBA ("doing business as" also called an "assumed name" or "fictitious name") that you'll use to have your fees paid to your LLC.

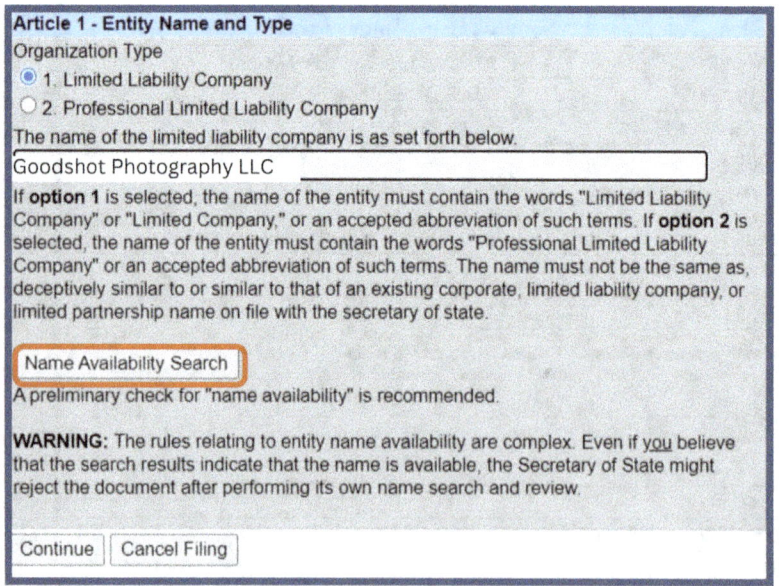

By the way, in case you were wondering, a Professional Limited Liability Company is specifically for professionals who require a state license to do business, like real estate agents, but there are some nuances with that type of entity that you may want to discuss with your attorney. The gist of it is that only licensed professionals may be owners of a PLLC, and although a PLLC cannot be used to shield the owner from malpractice claims, it does protect individual owners from being liable for the malpractice of the other owners, if there are multiple owners. Typically, if you're the only owner (or just you and your spouse), you don't need to form a PLLC. You would only do this if you were going to partner with another licensed professional in your business.

Another BTW, the owners of an LLC are technically referred to as "members", so we'll refer to them as such from now on to hopefully avoid any heartburn for us perfectionists in the room. 😁 Ok, on to the next screen!!

The name availability search results should show something resembling the following screenshot:

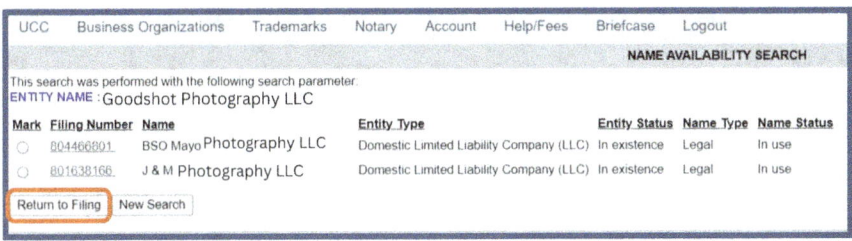

As long as there's not another business named Goodshot Photography LLC, or something very similar, you should be good to go and you can click the "Return to Filing" button, which should take you back to the previous screen with the name of your business that you entered. Click "Continue" at the bottom and you'll be prompted next to enter the mailing address.

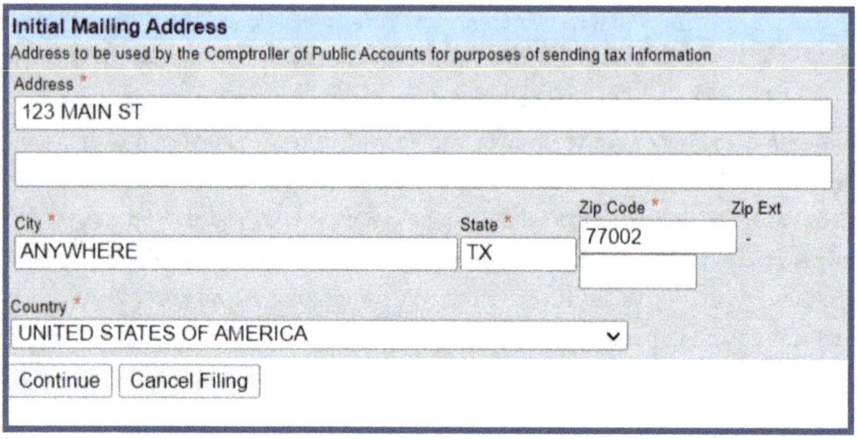

Initial Mailing Address

Address to be used by the Comptroller of Public Accounts for purposes of sending tax information

Address *

123 MAIN ST

City *	State *	Zip Code *	Zip Ext
ANYWHERE	TX	77002	-

Country *

UNITED STATES OF AMERICA

Continue   Cancel Filing

Next, you'll be asked to enter your "Registered Agent" name and address. The registered agent is basically a kind of liaison between your company and any state agencies, and some people will opt to pay a registered agent service (especially if they want some anonymity or if they're creating an out-of-state LLC where they have no physical presence, which is a level of complexity that we're not going to be covering in this ebook.)

The address used for the registered agent is where any official documents or notifications from those agencies are sent, so this MUST BE A PHYSICAL ADDRESS, it can't even be one of those UPS store addresses that looks like a physical address, so use your home or office address for this. You should name yourself as the registered agent to make sure you personally receive any of these important notifications. Otherwise, you can pay a third-party service anywhere from $35-$100 per year to serve as your registered agent. Select the "consent on file with entity" option, as you'll include that information in your Operating Agreement later.

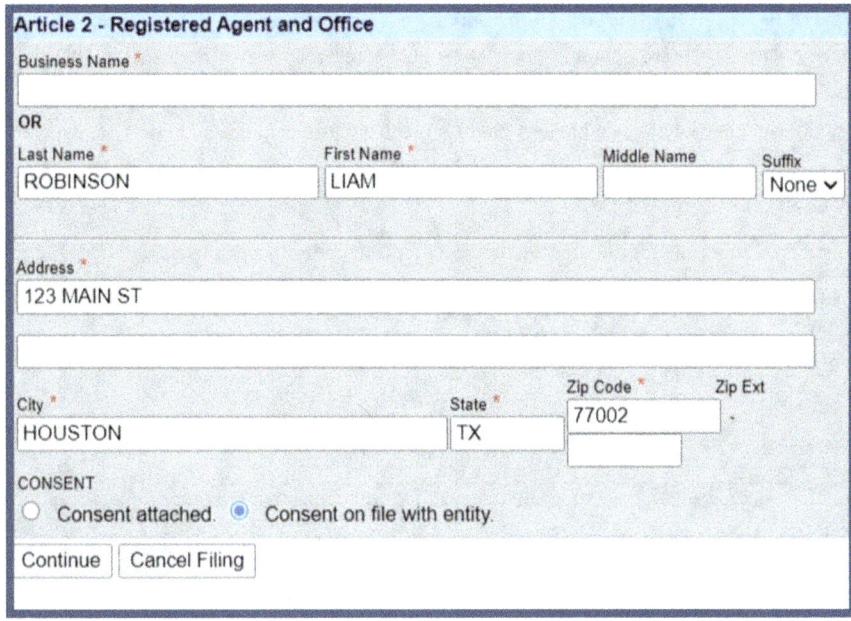

Article 2 - Registered Agent and Office

Business Name *

OR

Last Name *

ROBINSON

First Name *

LIAM

Middle Name

Suffix

None ▾

Address *

123 MAIN ST

City *

HOUSTON

State *

TX

Zip Code *

77002

Zip Ext

CONSENT

○ Consent attached. ● Consent on file with entity.

[Continue] [Cancel Filing]

Here you'll be asked for information about the "Governing Authority", which is just a fancy way of saying how your company will be managed. You have the option to elect managers that are not necessarily members (owners) of the company, who would run the day to day operations, but for your type of business, most likely that's just going to be you. So select the option for not having managers and then click the "Add Manager/Member" button.

Article 3 - Governing Authority

Management Type

○ The limited liability company is to be managed by managers. The names and addresses of the initial managers are set forth below:

● The limited liability company will not have managers. Management of the company is reserved to the members. The names and addresses of the initial members are set forth below:

Manager/Member Name and Address Information

Edit	Delete	Action	Name	Address
Add Manager/Member				

[Continue] [Cancel Filing]

Next you'll enter your personal information, leaving the Business Name section blank, as that's only if you're designating another business as an owner in your LLC. Fill out your name and address, click the "Update" button, and it will take you back to the previous screen only now showing your name as a member.

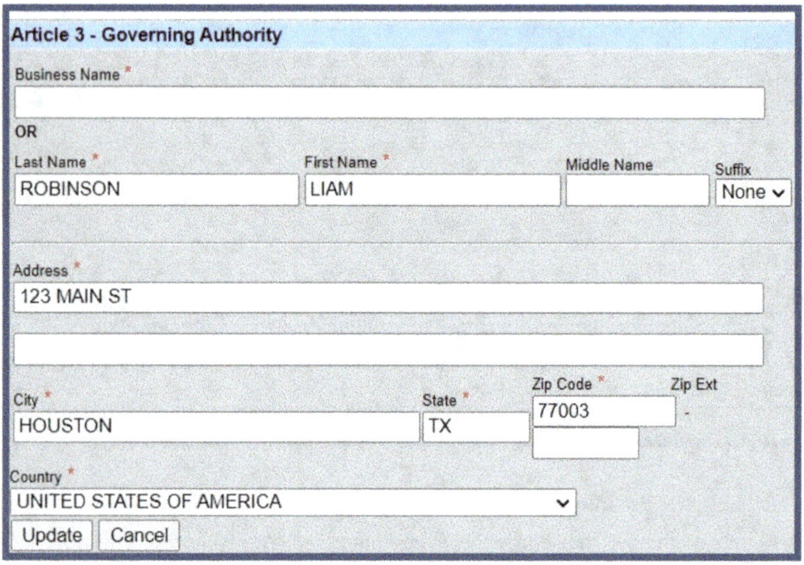

Article 3 - Governing Authority

Business Name *

OR

Last Name *	First Name *	Middle Name	Suffix
ROBINSON	LIAM		None ⌄

Address *

123 MAIN ST

City *	State *	Zip Code *	Zip Ext
HOUSTON	TX	77003	-

Country *

UNITED STATES OF AMERICA ⌄

[Update] [Cancel]

If you're married (or in a domestic partnership, or any other type of committed relationship), you might also consider adding your spouse/partner as a member and listing him/her as a signer on your bank account. That way if something were to happen to you, they would be able to access the funds in your account without going through an attorney. Although some of you may not want your significant other to have access to your business account, I'm going to leave that topic alone and let you hash that out amongst yourselves.

Special provisions don't need to be addressed here, as they'll be lined out in the sample Operating Agreement I've included, so you can just hit the "Continue" button.

Supplemental Provisions/Information

Reminder: A document filed with the Secretary of State is a public record. The document, and the information provided in the document, will be available online through SOSDirect for public viewing. Do not include confidential information, such as social security numbers, within a document or attachment. Use a business address rather than a residence address if privacy issues are a concern.

Attachment / Letter of Consent (SEE INSTRUCTIONS BELOW)

Delete	Choose File	No file chosen

Add Additional Attachments

Continue	Cancel Filing

You are the organizer, so enter your name and address here.

Organizer
The name and address of the organizer are set forth below.

Name	Address
LIAM ROBINSON	123 MAIN ST, HOUSTON, TX 77002

Continue	Cancel Filing

The next screen is a summary of all of the information you entered, so review it carefully for accuracy before submitting. If everything looks good, hit the "Submit Filing (Fee: $300.00)" button and it will file the documents for your LLC and charge your credit card. You should also see a confirmation screen, followed by an email confirmation.

Please review the document displayed for accuracy. If corrections must be made press 'Edit Filing'. When complete pre

Submit Filing (Fee: $300.00)   Edit Filing   Cancel Filing

Fees paid by credit card are subject to the statutorily authorized convenience fee of 2.7% of total fees.

Secretary of State
P.O. Box 13697
Austin, TX 78711-3697
FAX: 512/463-5709

Filing Fee: $300

**Certificate of Formation
Limited Liability Company**

Article 1 - Entity Name and Type

The filing entity being formed is a limited liability company. The name of the entity is:

Goodshot Photography LLC

Article 2 – Registered Agent and Registered Office

☐ A. The initial registered agent is an organization (cannot be company named above) by the name of:

OR

☑ B. The initial registered agent is an individual resident of the state whose name is set forth below:

Name:
IMA GOODSHOT

C. The business address of the registered agent and the registered office address is:

Street Address:
123 MAIN ST   HOUSTON TX 77002

Consent of Registered Agent

☐ A. A copy of the consent of registered agent is attached.

OR

☑ B. The consent of the registered agent is maintained by the entity.

Article 3 - Governing Authority

☐ A. The limited liability company is to be managed by managers.

OR

☑ B. The limited liability company will not have managers. Management of the company is reserved to the members.

The names and addresses of the governing persons are set forth below:

20

Managing Member 1: IMA GOODSHOT	Title: Managing Member

Address: 123 MAIN ST   HOUSTON TX, USA 77003

Article 4 - Purpose

The purpose for which the company is organized is for the transaction of any and all lawful business for which limited liability companies may be organized under the Texas Business Organizations Code.

Supplemental Provisions / Information

[The attached addendum, if any, is incorporated herein by reference]

Initial Mailing Address

Address to be used by the Comptroller of Public Accounts for purposes of sending tax information.

The initial mailing address of the filing entity is:
123 MAIN ST
HOUSTON, TX 77002
USA

Organizer

The name and address of the organizer are set forth below.
IMA GOODSHOT   123 MAIN ST, HOUSTON, TX 77002

Effectiveness of Filing

☑ A. This document becomes effective when the document is filed by the secretary of state.

OR

☐ B. This document becomes effective at a later date, which is not more than ninety (90) days from the date of its signing. The delayed effective date is:

Execution

The undersigned affirms that the person designated as registered agent has consented to the appointment. The undersigned signs this document subject to the penalties imposed by law for the submission of a materially false or fraudulent instrument and certifies under penalty of perjury that the undersigned is authorized under the provisions of law governing the entity to execute the filing instrument.

IMA GOODSHOT

Signature of Organizer

FILING OFFICE COPY

See, that wasn't as bad as you thought it would be, now was it? Now that you've completed the process with the SOS, it may take anywhere from 2 to 5 business days for them to process everything and mail/email your LLC documents to you, which would normally include a Certificate of Filing and Certificate of Formation (which is also called your Articles of Organization).

You may need to come back to this next part in a few days when you receive your Certificate of Filing from the SOS, as that will have your file number (see image below) that we'll need for requesting a DBA. But we'll go ahead and walk you through it here.

You may be asking "Why am I filing a DBA?" The reason is, some state licensing agencies (for example, TREC for real estate agents in Texas) will not allow you to receive commissions in the name of your LLC, but instead require that they be paid to the name of the person who is licensed, and since your LLC is not the one holding the license (even though for all practical purposes you and the LLC are the same), some brokers get caught up on this requirement and refuse to make an agent's commission check out to their LLC. But there's nothing saying that the broker is required to use the personal license holder's taxpayer number for 1099 reporting.

So you'll create a DBA that's actually "your name" under the LLC, and give your broker a W-9 (covered later in this ebook) that shows the name to make the checks out to (your name, which is also the DBA), and the LLCs EIN information for them to report on 1099 at the end of the year. Loophole for the win! 🙌

Ok, now that we've explained the why, let's cover the how. Whenever you have your file number, log back into the SOS site and go to the Business Organizations menu again. This time, you're going to enter the File Number and click the "File Document" button.

BUSINESS ORGANIZATIONS MENU	
CLIENT REFERENCE (optional): [NONE]	
● Client Reference: [ ]	Update Client Reference
INQUIRIES AND ORDERS	
● Name Availability Search	● Filing Number Search
● Find - Entity	● FEIN Search
● Find - Supplemental	● TID Search
● Find - Global	● Document Number Search
● Find - Assumed Name	● Order - Certificates and Copies
● Find - People	● Bulk Order - Data
● Find - Registered Agent	● Registered Agent activity past 60 days
WEB FILINGS	

DO NOT USE 'BACK' BUTTON
Use of the 'BACK' button during the "WEB FILINGS" process will result in loss of data. Please press the 'Cancel Filing' button and start again.

● Reservation ˅ Formation ˅ Registration Documents
First select the type of entity for which you wish to submit a filing, and then click 'File Document'
[Application for Name Reservation ▾]   [File Document]

File assumed name certificates, changes to registered office/agent, dissolutions, reinstatements, cancellations, withdrawals and annual statements as change documents.

● Change Documents
Enter filing number and click 'File Document' or click 'Find Entity'
[123412341234]   [Find Entity]   [File Document]

● Master Filing
● Master Filing Search/Cost Estimator

You should see on the next screen your entity name and "In Existence" as the status. In the "Filing Type" drop-down, select "Certificate of Assumed Business Name" and click "Continue".

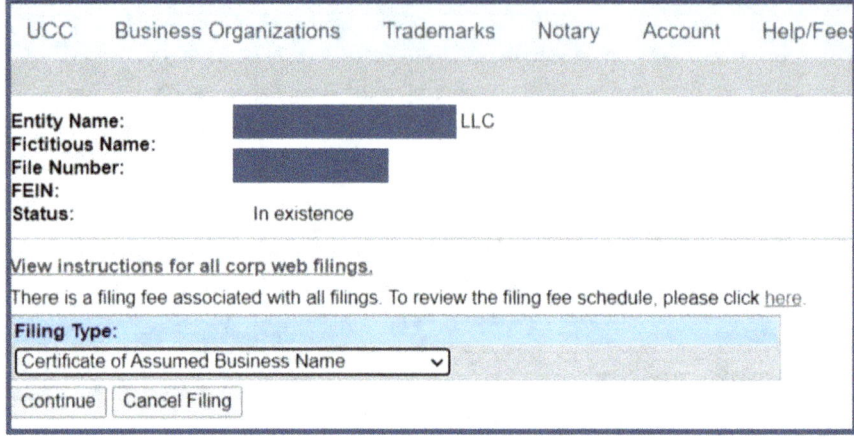

On the next screen, enter your legal name as reflected on your real estate license.

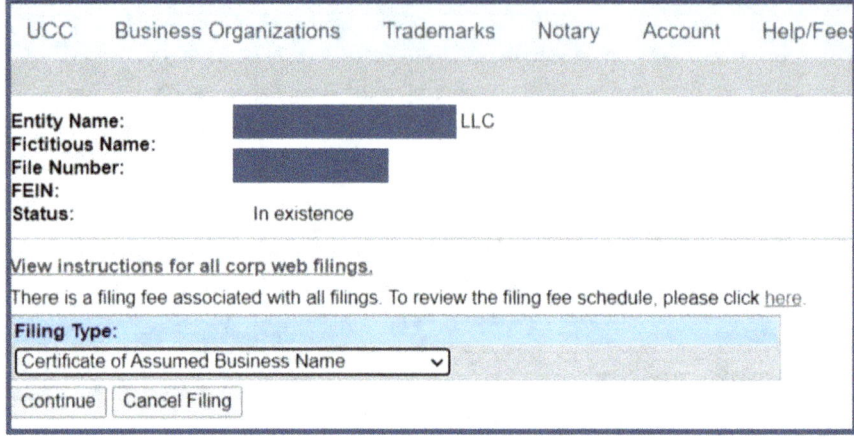

In Texas, a DBA only lasts for 10 years, so enter today's date plus 10 years here.

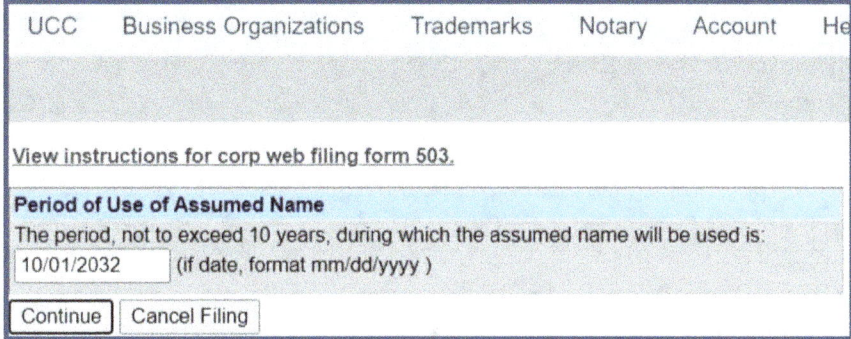

Select either "All Counties" or a specific county that you're operating in. You may also select multiple counties that are in your area that you anticipate covering in your real estate practice. There usually isn't an additional fee for more counties.

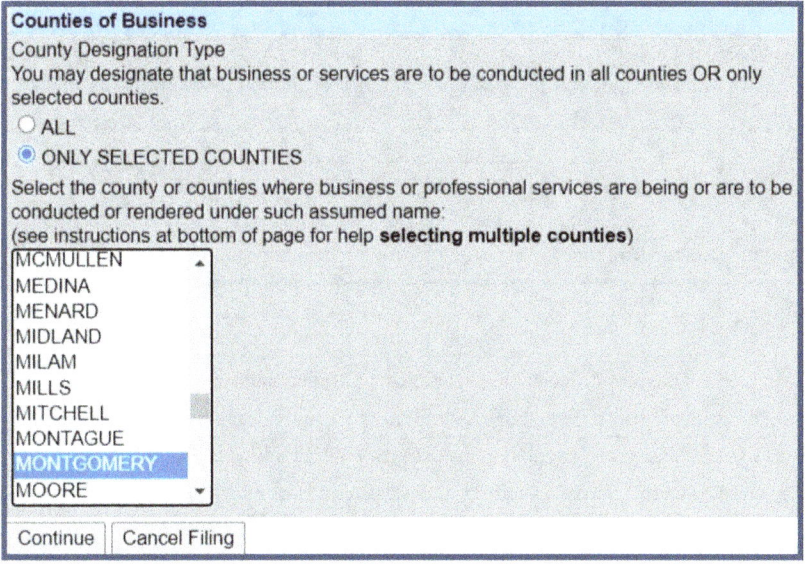

Enter your business address here.

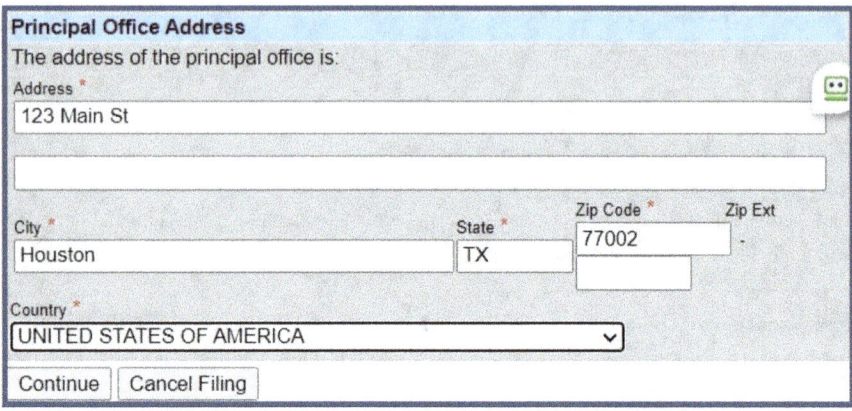

Enter your name as the signature.

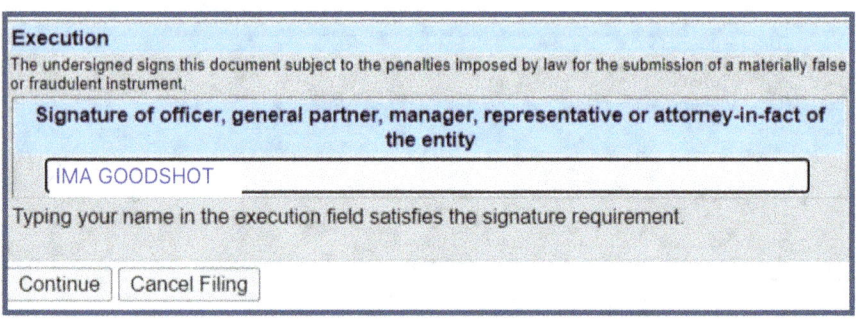

The last page is a summary, so review the information to make sure it's all correct, then hit the "Submit Filing (Fee: $25)" button at the top of the page. Similar to when you filed for the LLC, you'll receive a confirmation email and within a few days another email with the actual Certificate of Assumed Name for the LLC.

Please review the document displayed for accuracy. If corrections must be made press 'Edit Filing'. When con

Submit Filing (Fee: $25.00) | Edit Filing | Cancel Filing

Fees paid by credit card are subject to the statutorily authorized convenience fee of 2.7% of total fees

There are some fields displayed in the document by retrieving information from the SOS database, such as registered agent and office. T
following the submission of the assumed name certificate

Office of the Secretary of State
Corporations Section
P.O. Box 13697
Austin, Texas 78711-3697
(Form 503)

ASSUMED NAME CERTIFICATE
FOR FILING WITH THE SECRETARY OF STATE

1. The assumed name under which the business or professional service is or is to be conducted or rendered is:

IMA GOODSHOT

2. The name of the entity as stated in its certificate of formation, application for registration, or comparable document is:

3. The state, country, or other jurisdiction under the laws of which it was incorporated, organized or associated is TEXAS

4. The period, not to exceed 10 years, during which the assumed name will be used is :
10/01/2032

Now you're ready for step #2, which involves filing a few items with the IRS to ensure you're on your way to magnanimous tax savings.

Step 2: File Other Critical Forms with the IRS

The next few steps involve applying for a Federal Employer Identification Number (EIN) and then filing Form 2553 in which you elect to have the business treated as an S-Corporation. Filing Form 2553 with the IRS is critical if you're going to achieve maximum tax savings, otherwise, all of the income that goes through the LLC is taxed at the additional 15%, defeating its entire purpose.

Now, don't ask me why, but for some strange reason, the portion of the IRS website where you go to apply for an EIN is only available during the following hours:
Monday - Friday: 7:00 a.m. to 10:00 p.m. Eastern time
Saturday: Closed
Sunday: Closed

Leave it up to the IRS to be the only operating entity in the world to "close their website" at night and on the weekends. I guess they have to allow their little EIN- processing gnomes to rest for a few hours every night or they'll quit and go to work for Travelocity or some other more exciting place. I really don't know...

Okay, so if you happen to be reading this ebook during those hours, go ahead and **click here** to go to the IRS website and then click the "Begin Application" button. Otherwise, you'll have to come back during the daylight hours.

Here's what you'll see when you click the link above:

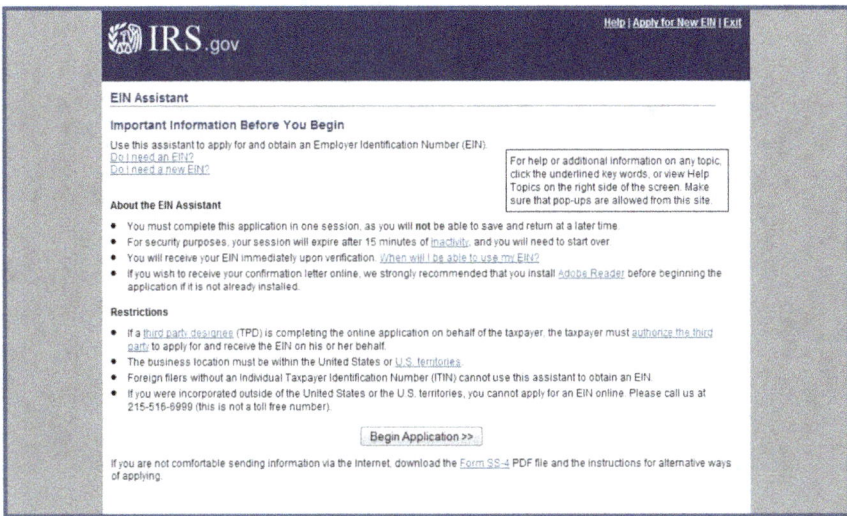

The first question is pretty self-explanatory, as you'll be creating an LLC.

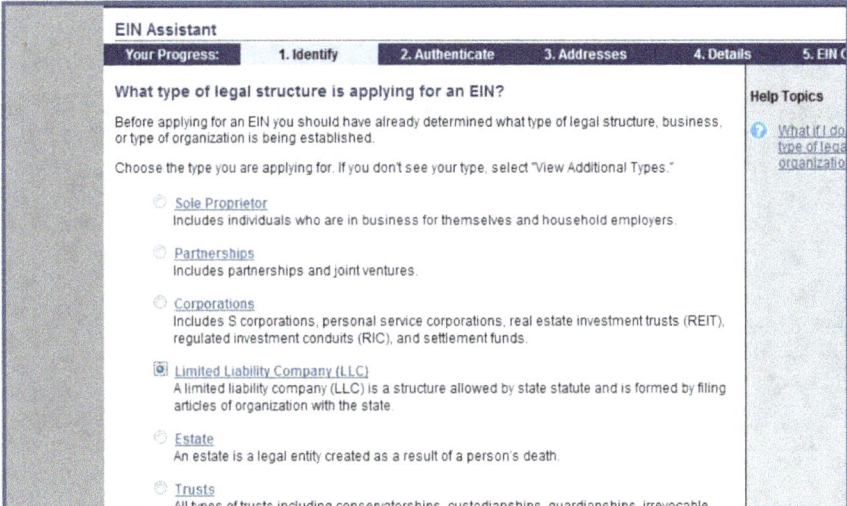

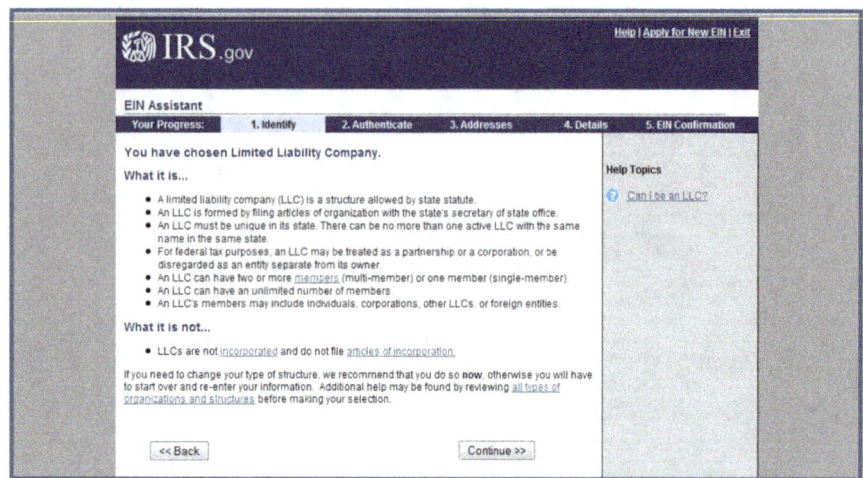

If you indicate on this next screenshot that your LLC will only have 1 member, it's going to tell you about some options as far as how you want the IRS to treat the LLC for tax purposes.

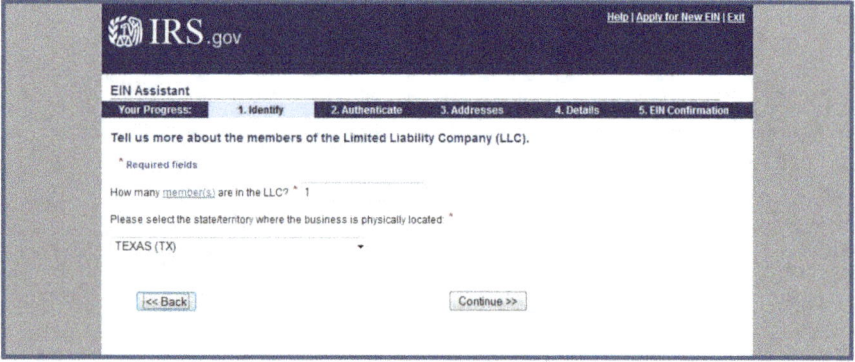

By default, a single-member LLC is treated as a "Disregarded Entity" as far as the IRS is concerned. This is sort of like being called a "red-headed stepchild" in some ways, because you don't get any kind of preferential treatment this way, at least not for tax purposes. (No offense to all you red-headed step children out there, we really do love all the gingers!)

If the IRS treats your LLC like a red-headed Disregarded Entity, all of the income that flows through the LLC gets hit with the 15% self- employment tax. This is not what you want. Don't worry, once you've finished with your EIN, I'll tell you how to get preferential tax treatment by filling out Form 2553. So all you need to do here is click on the "Continue" button.

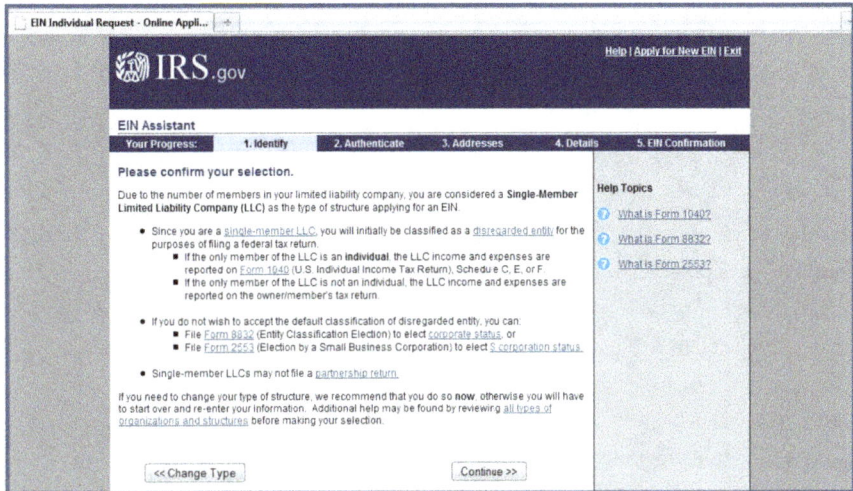

Going back to the previous question, if you indicate that your LLC will have 2 members, and that those members are husband and wife living in a community property state, you'll see the following screen:

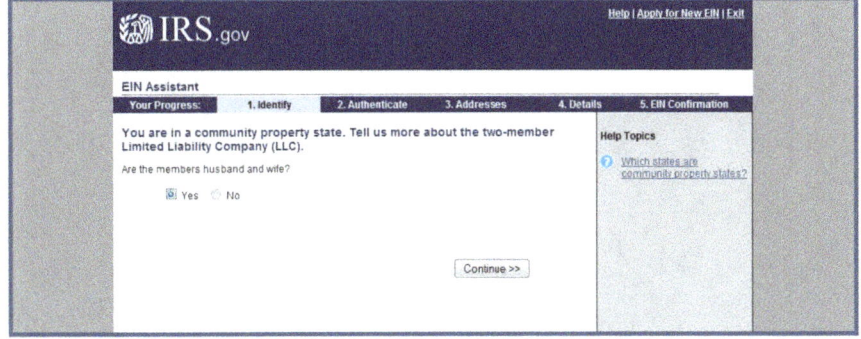

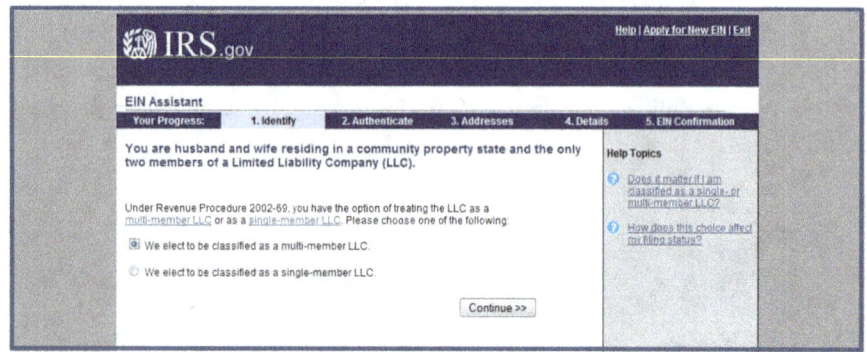

The way you answer the above question is crucial to how the income flowing through your LLC gets taxed. If you elect to be classified as a single-member LLC, you get the Disregarded Entity tax treatment, aka "red-headed stepchild". So you want to make sure you tell the IRS to treat you as a multi-member LLC at this point, and they'll treat you like a partnership. However, even as a partnership, you still get hit with the 15% self-employment tax on all of your income (they really try to make it hard to avoid that 15%, don't they?), so you still need to file Form 2553 also, which I'll get to in just a few minutes. See how confusing all this can become rather quickly? Now, aren't you glad you bought this ebook?

Now, for this next question, if you're a brand new agent just starting out, you can select the "Started a new business" option. Otherwise, you'll select the "Changed type of organization" option, since you'll be changing from being a sole-proprietor filing a Schedule C on your 1040, to being a separate legal entity altogether.

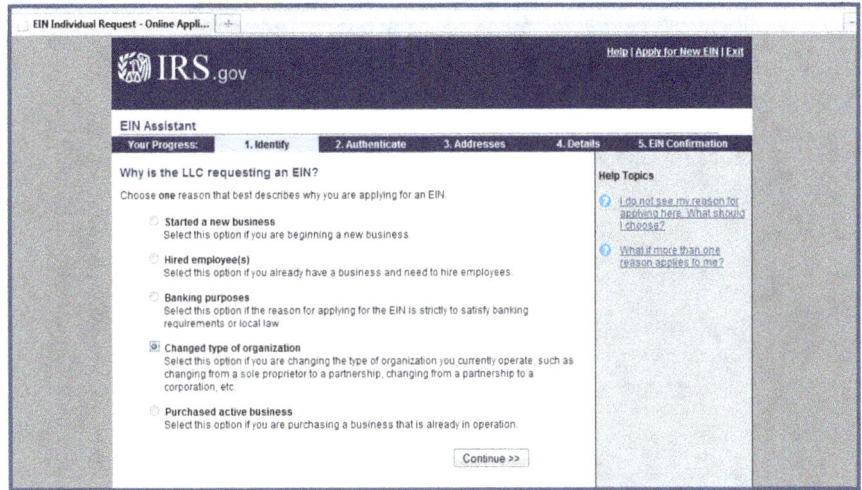

Now here you're just telling the IRS that you are the person who is taking ultimate responsibility for your LLC.

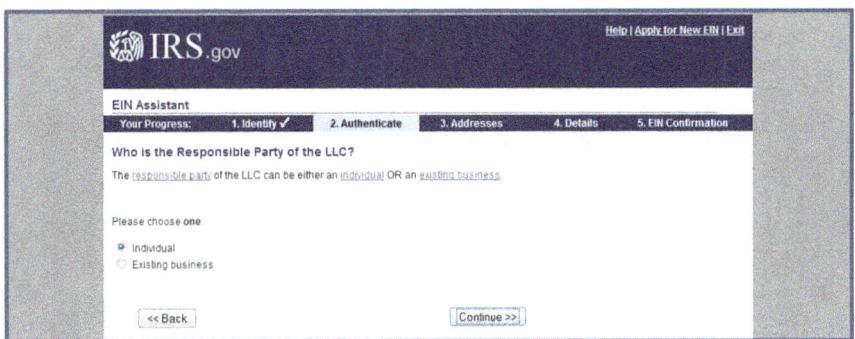

Since you are applying for your own LLC, you'll provide info about yourself on the next screen.

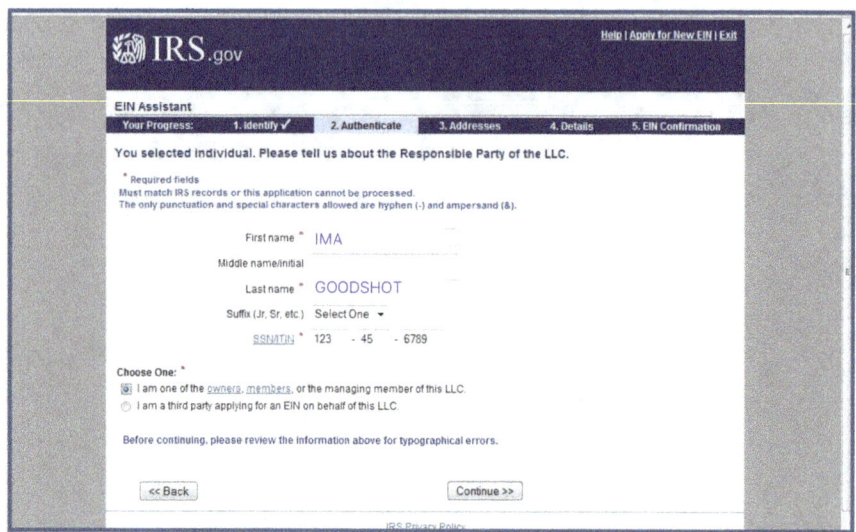

I would recommend using your home address, rather than the office address of a firm you may be contracting with. That way, if you ever go to work for another firm, you won't have to worry about changing the address for your LLC.

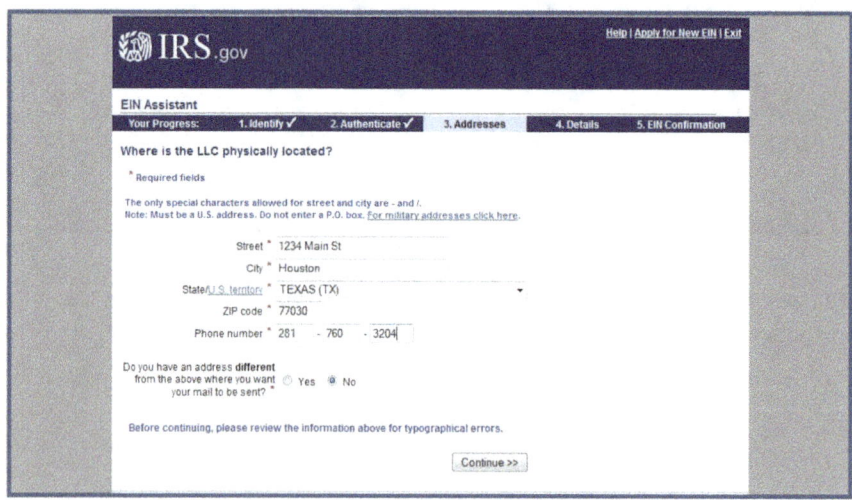

Enter your new LLC name as the legal name and the DBA as the trade name. The LLC start date is just the month and year you set up your LLC, presumably this month.

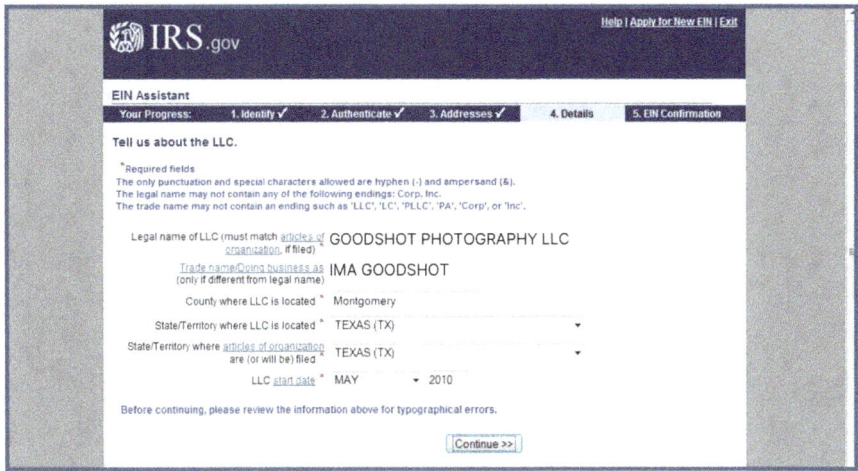

None of these questions apply, except the last one, as you'll be hiring yourself.

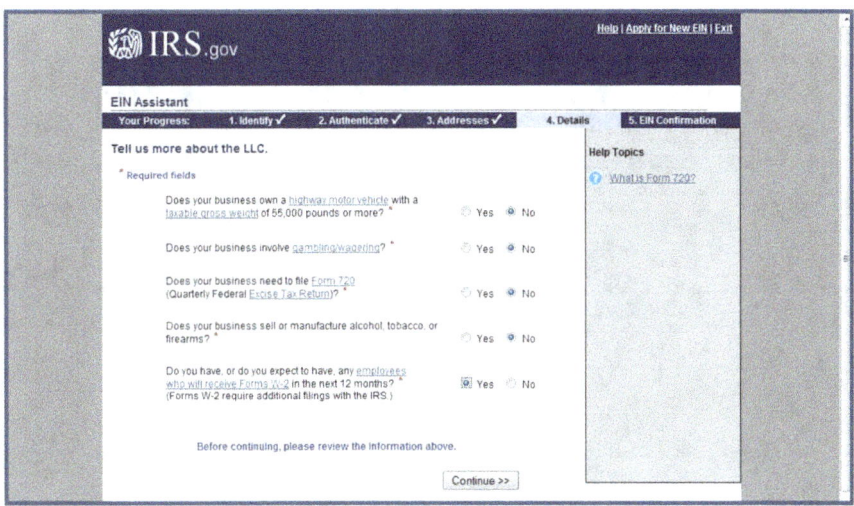

I recommend indicating next month as the first date salaries will be paid. And I would select "No" to indicate that you expect your employment tax liability will not be $1,000 or less.

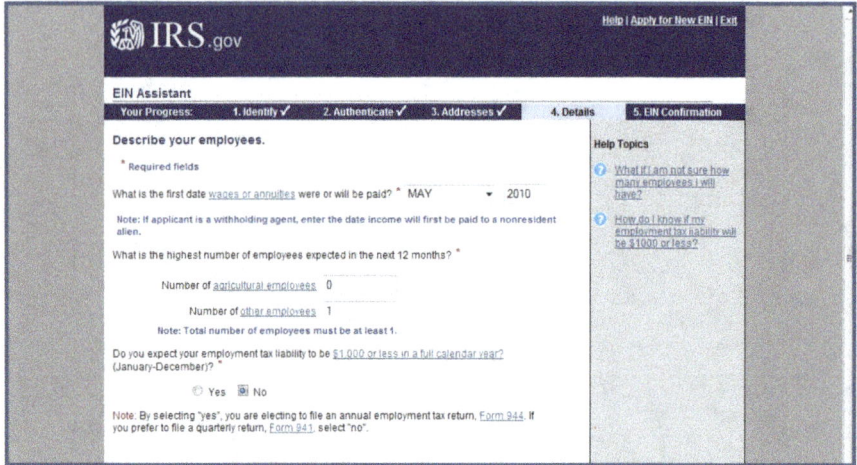

For this question, select the closest option or "other". (Screenshot continued on the next page.)

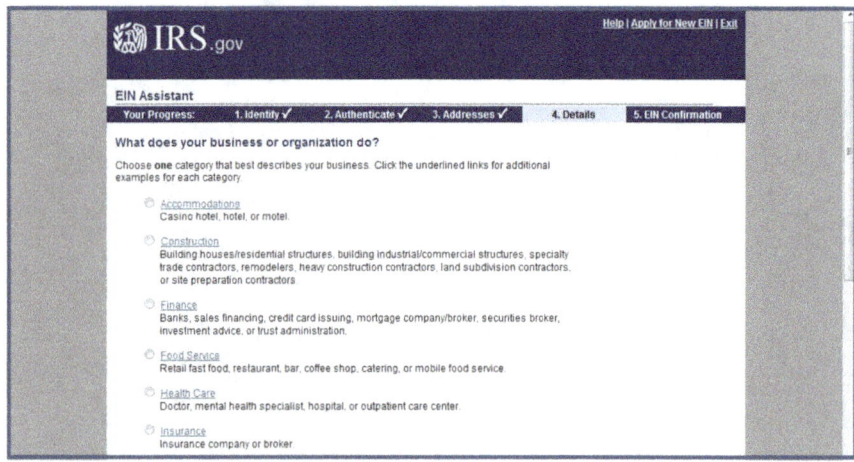

○ Real Estate
Renting or leasing real estate, managing real estate, real estate agent/broker, selling, buying, or renting real estate for others.

○ Rental & Leasing
Rent/lease automobiles, consumer goods, commercial goods, or industrial goods.

○ Retail
Retail store, internet sales (exclusively), direct sales (catalogue, mail-order, door to door), auction house, or selling goods on auction sites.

○ Social Assistance
Youth services, residential care facility, services for the disabled, or community food/housing/relief services.

○ Transportation
Air transportation, rail transportation, water transportation, trucking, passenger transportation, support activity for transportation, or delivery/courier service.

○ Warehousing
Operating warehousing or storage facilities for general merchandise, refrigerated goods, or other warehouse products, establishments that provide facilities to store goods but do not sell the goods they handle.

○ Wholesale
Wholesale agent/broker, importer, exporter, manufacturers' representative, merchant, distributor, or jobber.

● Other

[<< Back]   [Continue >>]

IRS Privacy Policy | Accessibility

You have chosen Other.

Please choose **one** of the following that best describes your primary business activity:

○ Consulting

○ Manufacturing

○ Organization (such as religious, environmental, social or civic, athletic, etc.)

○ Rental

○ Repair

○ Sell goods

● Service

○ Other – please specify your primary business activity:

[   ]

You have chosen Other: Service.

What is the primary service you provide?

[PHOTOGRAPHY   ]

[Continue >>]

Here you'll want to receive your letter online, which will allow you to view your EIN immediately after viewing the summary page (next screenshot), otherwise, it could take up to four weeks to receive it in the mail.

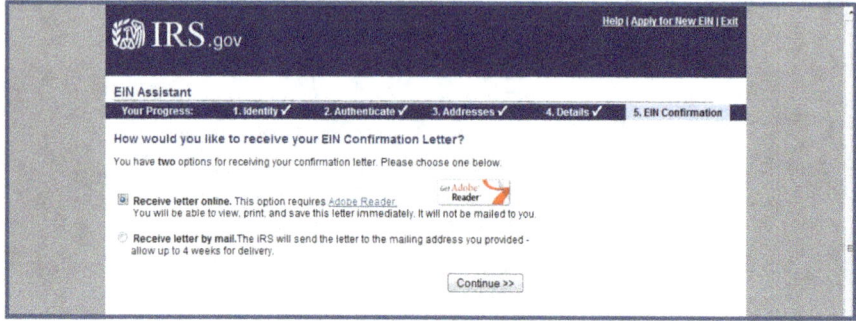

The next screenshot is the summary page, so make sure to review it all carefully, make any changes if necessary, then click the "Submit" button.

IRS.gov

EIN Assistant

Your Progress:	1. Identity ✓	2. Authenticate ✓	3. Addresses ✓	4. Details ✓	5. EIN Confirmation

Summary of your information

Please review the information you are about to submit. If any of the information below is incorrect, you will need to start a new application.

Click the "Submit" button at the bottom of the page to receive your EIN.

Help Topics

? What is Form 11287

Organization Type: LLC

LLC Information

Legal name	**GOODSHOT PHOTOGRAPHY LLC**
County	MONTGOMERY
State/Territory	TX
Start date	MAY 2010
Closing month of accounting year	DECEMBER (The closing month of the accounting year is defaulted to December due to your organization type. To change your closing month of accounting year, complete Form 1128.)
State/Territory where articles of organization are (or will be) filed	TX

Addresses

Physical Location:	THE WOODLANDS TX 77380
Phone Number:	

Responsible Party

Name:	**IMA GOODSHOT MBR**
SSN/ITIN:	

Employee Information

Date wages or annuities will be paid	MAY 2010
Number of agricultural employees	0
Number of other employees	1
Tax Liability of $1000 or less during calendar year	NO

Principal Business Activity

What your business/organization does	**SERVICE**
Principal products/services	**PHOTOGRAPHY**

Additional LLC Information

Owns a 55,000 pounds or greater highway motor vehicle	NO
Involves gambling/wagering	NO
Involves alcohol, tobacco or firearms	NO
Files Form 720 (Quarterly Federal Excise Tax Return)	NO
Has employees who receive Forms W-2	YES
Reason for Applying	CHANGED TYPE OF ORGANIZATION

We strongly recommend you print this summary page for your records as this will be your only copy of the application. You will not be able to return to this page after you click the "Submit" button.

Click "Submit" to send your request and receive your EIN. [Submit] Once you submit, please wait while your application is being processed. It can take up to two minutes for your application to be processed.

IRS Privacy Policy

39

Now, instead of just clicking the link that says "CLICK HERE for your EIN Confirmation Letter", click your right mouse button on the link to bring up the following menu. If you click "Save Link As..." it gives you the option to save the EIN confirmation letter in PDF form before opening it. Sometimes, depending on your browser, and depending on what kind of mood your computer is in that day, I've seen it mess up and not open the EIN confirmation letter if you click directly on the link. At least now you have the document saved to your hard drive if it decides it doesn't want you to see your EIN letter when you click the link.

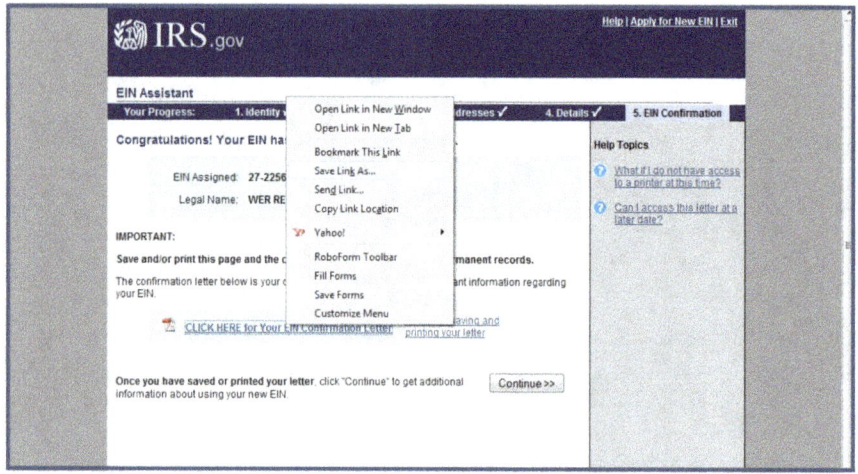

After you've right-clicked and saved the document, go ahead and click the link (make sure you cross your fingers, too!), and Voila! There's your EIN confirmation letter with your EIN in the top right-hand corner.

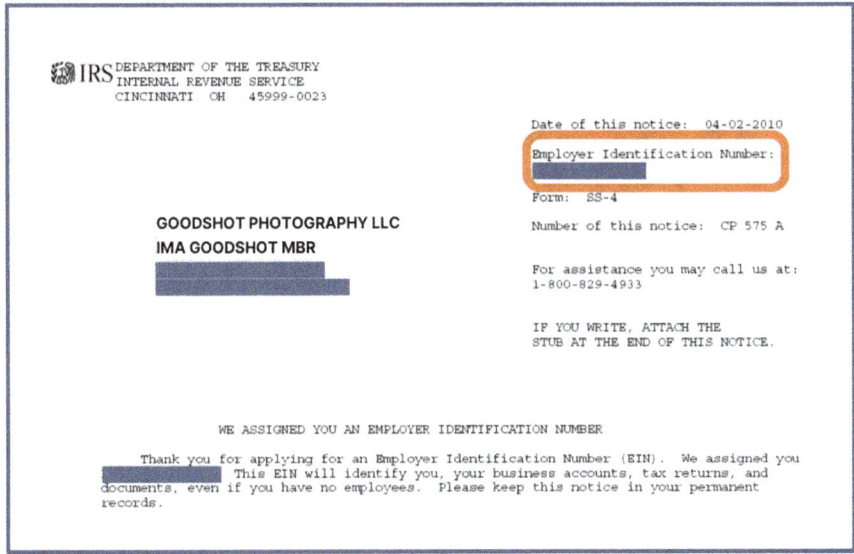

Please note that the EIN confirmation letter states that you must file form 1065 because the IRS initially treats the LLC as a partnership by default. However, once they receive and process your Form 2553 (up next in this here DIY manual), you'll receive another letter from the IRS letting you know that they've accepted your request to be taxed as an S-Corporation and, as such, you'll now be required to file Form 1120S instead of Form 1065. This is the business version of your 1040 tax return, which will allow you to no longer file a Schedule C and be a much smaller target for the IRS audit bullies.

This next page is just going to tell you what you can do with your new EIN. Here's where you'll want to click on the link that says "Form 2553" and fill it out using the sample form I've provided on the next page.

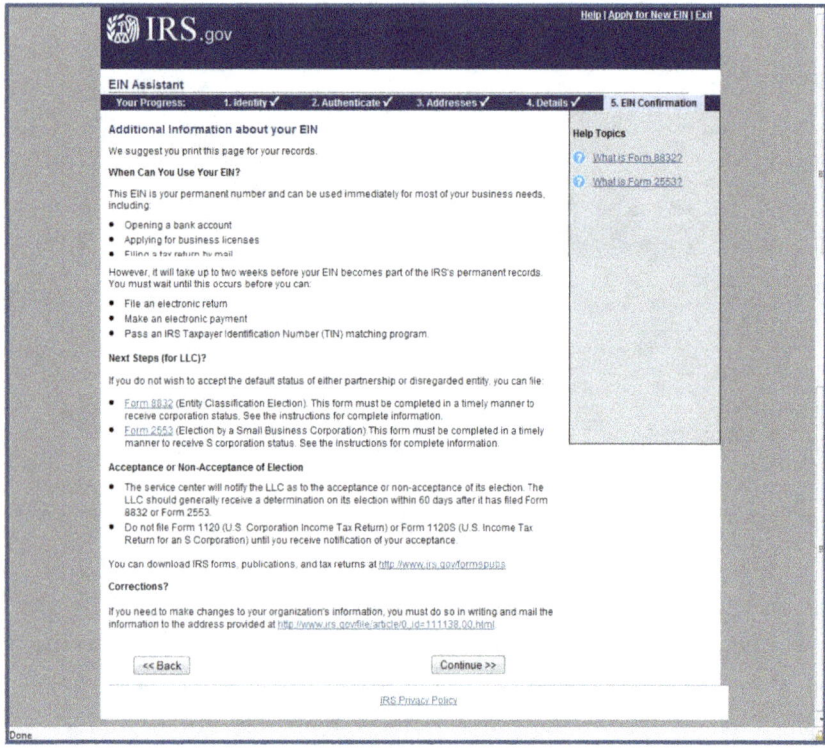

You can also **click this link** to go to Form 2553. Look at the sample form below to see how to fill it out correctly.

Link: http://www.irs.gov/pub/irs-pdf/f2553.pdf

Form **2553**
(Rev. December 2017)
Department of the Treasury
Internal Revenue Service

Election by a Small Business Corporation
(Under section 1362 of the Internal Revenue Code)
(Including a late election filed pursuant to Rev. Proc. 2013-30)

▶ You can fax this form to the IRS. See separate instructions.
▶ Go to *www.irs.gov/Form2553* for instructions and the latest information.

OMB No. 1545-0123

Note: This election to be an S corporation can be accepted only if all the tests are met under *Who May Elect* in the instructions. all shareholders have signed the consent statement, an officer has signed below, and the exact name and address of the corporation (entity) and other required form information have been provided.

Part I   Election Information

Type or Print	Name (see instructions) GOODSHOT PHOTOGRAPHY LLC	**A** Employer identification number 12-46545615
	Number, street, and room or suite no. If a P.O. box, see instructions. 1234 MAIN STREET	**B** Date incorporated 01/01/2023
	City or town, state or province, country, and ZIP or foreign postal code HOUSTON, TX, USA, 77080	**C** State of incorporation TEXAS

D Check the applicable box(es) if the corporation (entity), after applying for the EIN shown in **A** above, changed its ☐ name or ☐ address

E Election is to be effective for tax year beginning (month, day, year) (see instructions) . . . . ▶ 01/01/2023

Caution: A corporation (entity) making the election for its first tax year in existence will usually enter the beginning date of a short tax year that begins on a date other than January 1.

F Selected tax year:
(1) ☑ Calendar year
(2) ☐ Fiscal year ending (month and day) ▶ _____
(3) ☐ 52-53-week year ending with reference to the month of December
(4) ☐ 52-53-week year ending with reference to the month of ▶ _____
If box (2) or (4) is checked, complete Part II.

G If more than 100 shareholders are listed for item J (see page 2), check this box if treating members of a family as one shareholder results in no more than 100 shareholders (see test 2 under *Who May Elect* in the instructions) ▶ ☐

H Name and title of officer or legal representative whom the IRS may call for more information IMA GOODSHOT, MANAGING MEMBER	Telephone number of officer or legal representative 713-867-5309

I If this S corporation election is being filed late, I declare I had reasonable cause for not filing Form 2553 timely. If this late election is being made by an entity eligible to elect to be treated as a corporation, I declare I also had reasonable cause for not filing an entity classification election timely and the representations listed in Part IV are true. See below for my explanation of the reasons the election or elections were not made on time and a description of my diligent actions to correct the mistake upon its discovery. See instructions.

Sign Here ▶	Under penalties of perjury, I declare that I have examined this election, including accompanying documents, and, to the best of my knowledge and belief, the election contains all the relevant facts relating to the election, and such facts are true, correct, and complete.

Signature of officer	Title MANAGING MEMBER	Date

For Paperwork Reduction Act Notice, see separate instructions.   Cat. No. 18629R   Form **2553** (Rev. 12-2017)

For questions B and E, your tax year begins on the date you incorporate, so you can use the date that you applied for the LLC with the SOS, even though it does take 2-3 days to process the filing documents with the state. If the date you enter on Form 2553 is off by a few days from the actual incorporation date, it's okay, this will not affect your treatment as an S-Corporation. You'll also use this same date on page 2, column L "Date Acquired".

Form 2553 (Rev. 12-2017)   Page **2**

Name	Employer identification number
GOODSHOT PHOTOGRAPHY LLC	12-4654561

Part I   Election Information *(continued)* Note: If you need more rows, use additional copies of page 2.

J Name and address of each shareholder or former shareholder required to consent to the election. (see instructions)	K Shareholder's Consent Statement Under penalties of perjury, I declare that I consent to the election of the above-named corporation (entity) to be an S corporation under section 1362(a) and that I have examined this consent statement, including accompanying documents, and, to the best of my knowledge and belief, the election contains all the relevant facts relating to the election, and such facts are true, correct, and complete. I understand my consent is binding and may not be withdrawn after the corporation (entity) has made a valid election. If seeking relief for a late filed election, I also declare under penalties of perjury that I have reported my income on all affected returns consistent with the S corporation election for the year for which the election should have been filed (see beginning date entered on line E) and for all subsequent years.		L Stock owned or percentage of ownership (see instructions)		M Social security number or employer identification number (see instructions)	N Shareholder's tax year ends (month and day)
	Signature	Date	Number of shares or percentage of ownership	Date(s) acquired		
IMA GOODSHOT 1234 MAIN STREET HOUSTON, TX 77080		01/01/2023	50%	01/01/2023	123-45-6789	12/31
ANITA GOODSHOT 1234 MAIN STREET HOUSTON, TX 77080		01/01/2023	50%	01/01/2023	123-45-9876	12/31

Form **2553** (Rev. 12-2017)

There are 2 more pages of the form, and even though none of it applies to your situation so you don't need to fill any of those pages out, you should still enter your business name and EIN at the top of each page and mail in all of the pages together, otherwise, the IRS may think it's incomplete and send you a nasty denial letter.

Once you've filled out Form 2553, be sure to sign and date in column K as well as at the bottom next to where it says "Signature of Officer". Then mail or fax it (if you're 100 years old) to the IRS office below based on the state in which your LLC is located:

If the corporation's principal business, office, or agency is located in:	Use the following address or fax number:
Connecticut, Delaware, District of Columbia, Georgia, Illinois, Indiana, Kentucky, Maine, Maryland, Massachusetts, Michigan, New Hampshire, New Jersey, New York, North Carolina, Ohio, Pennsylvania, Rhode Island, South Carolina, Tennessee, Vermont, Virginia, West Virginia, Wisconsin	Department of the Treasury Internal Revenue Service Center Kansas City, MO 64999 Fax: 855-887-7734
Alabama, Alaska, Arizona, Arkansas, California, Colorado, Florida, Hawaii, Idaho, Iowa, Kansas, Louisiana, Minnesota, Mississippi, Missouri, Montana, Nebraska, Nevada, New Mexico, North Dakota, Oklahoma, Oregon, South Dakota, Texas, Utah, Washington, Wyoming	Department of the Treasury Internal Revenue Service Center Ogden, UT 84201 Fax: 855-214-7520

IMPORTANT NOTE:
It's absolutely critical that you send this form in to the IRS within 60 days of establishing your LLC, so go ahead and do it now before you forget! I also recommend mailing it Certified with the Return Receipt Requested so you receive proof of when it was mailed and received.

Congratulations! You've set up your very own LLC! Now that we've gotten that taken care of, let's talk about how to conduct business with your new LLC.

Step 3:
Open a Bank Account

Now that you've established your LLC, the IRS wants to make sure that you're not just "living out of your business bank account." In other words, they don't want to see you paying all of your personal expenses out of the business account. So we want to make sure you keep business expenses separate from your personal expenses.

The documents you'll receive from the Secretary of State's office include your Certificate of Filing, your Articles of Incorporation, and your Certificate of Assumed Name. These documents along with your EIN letter from the IRS are what your bank will typically want to see in order to open up a business bank account. Sometimes they'll also want a copy of the LLC Operating Agreement, which is also included in this book's Appendix.

And just to make the point again, I recommend listing your spouse as a signer on the bank account, just in case if you were to get run over by a turnip truck one day, your spouse would have access to those funds more easily.

Once you've opened up a business bank account, you'll want to provide your broker or contracting firm with a Form W-9, which instructs them to start reporting your commissions under the new LLCs EIN, instead of your SSN. Form W-9 can be downloaded by **clicking here**, and it simply asks for your name (which is the LLCs name), business name (which is your DBA), address and EIN. I know that the last part I said about your name being the name of the LLC and your business name being the DBA may sound backward, but trust me, this is how the actual IRS instructions specify that you enter this information. The broker / firm will be making payments to whatever name is in the business name field, so you want that to be your DBA. Oh, and make sure you select the checkbox next to "Limited Liability Corporation" and enter "S" at the end of the same line in section 3 of the form. This form doesn't need to be filed with the IRS, it only needs to be given to the requestor (whoever is paying you) to confirm your tax information for when they send you a 1099 at the end of the year.

Link: http://www.irs.gov/pub/irs-pdf/fw9.pdf

Form W-9
(Rev. October 2018)
Department of the Treasury
Internal Revenue Service

Request for Taxpayer Identification Number and Certification

▶ Go to *www.irs.gov/FormW9* for instructions and the latest information.

Give Form to the requester. Do not send to the IRS.

1 Name (as shown on your income tax return). Name is required on this line; do not leave this line blank.
GOODSHOT PHOTOGRAPHY LLC

2 Business name/disregarded entity name, if different from above
IMA GOODSHOT

3 Check appropriate box for federal tax classification of the person whose name is entered on line 1. Check only **one** of the following seven boxes.

☐ Individual/sole proprietor or single-member LLC ☐ C Corporation ☐ S Corporation ☐ Partnership ☐ Trust/estate

☑ Limited liability company. Enter the tax classification (C=C corporation, S=S corporation, P=Partnership) ▶ **S**

Note: Check the appropriate box in the line above for the tax classification of the single-member owner. Do not check LLC if the LLC is classified as a single-member LLC that is disregarded from the owner unless the owner of the LLC is another LLC that is **not** disregarded from the owner for U.S. federal tax purposes. Otherwise, a single-member LLC that is disregarded from the owner should check the appropriate box for the tax classification of its owner.

☐ Other (see instructions) ▶

4 Exemptions (codes apply only to certain entities, not individuals; see instructions on page 3):

Exempt payee code (if any) _____

Exemption from FATCA reporting code (if any) _____

(Applies to accounts maintained outside the U.S.)

5 Address (number, street, and apt. or suite no.) See instructions.
123 MAIN ST

6 City, state, and ZIP code
HOUSTON, TX 77002

7 List account number(s) here (optional)

Requester's name and address (optional)

Part I **Taxpayer Identification Number (TIN)**

Enter your TIN in the appropriate box. The TIN provided must match the name given on line 1 to avoid backup withholding. For individuals, this is generally your social security number (SSN). However, for a resident alien, sole proprietor, or disregarded entity, see the instructions for Part I, later. For other entities, it is your employer identification number (EIN). If you do not have a number, see *How to get a TIN*, later.

Note: If the account is in more than one name, see the instructions for line 1. Also see *What Name and Number To Give the Requester* for guidelines on whose number to enter.

Social security number
☐☐☐ - ☐☐ - ☐☐☐☐

or

Employer identification number
2 6 - 1 2 3 4 5 6 7

Part II **Certification**

Under penalties of perjury, I certify that:

1. The number shown on this form is my correct taxpayer identification number (or I am waiting for a number to be issued to me); and
2. I am not subject to backup withholding because: (a) I am exempt from backup withholding, or (b) I have not been notified by the Internal Revenue Service (IRS) that I am subject to backup withholding as a result of a failure to report all interest or dividends, or (c) the IRS has notified me that I am no longer subject to backup withholding; and
3. I am a U.S. citizen or other U.S. person (defined below); and
4. The FATCA code(s) entered on this form (if any) indicating that I am exempt from FATCA reporting is correct.

Certification instructions. You must cross out item 2 above if you have been notified by the IRS that you are currently subject to backup withholding because you have failed to report all interest and dividends on your tax return. For real estate transactions, item 2 does not apply. For mortgage interest paid,

So now that you've got the business bank account set up and you're depositing your checks into that account, how do you take money out for your personal expenses without being gouged by the IRS? I'm glad you asked...because the vast majority of small business owners make the mistake of paying personal expenses directly out of their LLC bank account, something the IRS calls "commingling of funds" which can quickly result in the IRS disallowing certain business expenses. So let's next discuss some ways to properly take money out of your LLC.

Step 4: Pay Yourself a "Reasonable" Salary

As an LLC that's taxed as an S-Corporation, the IRS requires you to pay the owners (that's you) what they refer to as "reasonable compensation". There's no specific guidance from the IRS as to what they consider "reasonable", but as a real estate agent, you can easily argue that a $20,000-30,000 salary is reasonable, especially if you're just starting out. A good rule of thumb is to take your average monthly income from your business minus your average monthly expenses, multiply that times 12, and whatever that number comes out to, multiply it times 25%, and that's a good "reasonable" salary to pay yourself. Now remember that although that may seem like a really small amount, this is the only amount that's going to be subject to the 15% self-employment tax, so you actually want your salary to be as small as possible.

Okay, now that you've determined your salary, let's talk about what's involved when you pay yourself a salary; because in the eyes of the IRS and your state, your LLC is now an employer (and you are the employee).

As an employer, when your LLC pays someone a salary, it's required to withhold payroll taxes from the paycheck, and those withheld taxes must be paid either quarterly or monthly. Your LLC is required to file quarterly payroll reports with the IRS, and depending on your state, you may be required to withhold state income tax and file state payroll reports either monthly or quarterly.

The best way to cut through all of the confusion of keeping up with how much payroll tax is due and when, who to pay, and what forms to file, is to outsource that job to an expert in payroll matters. The good news is that I've already found a source for you that's the most user-friendly, hassle-free way for handling all of this payroll stuff, and you are guaranteed 100% accuracy and timely filing of reports. In other words, you never have to mess with the headache of managing your own payroll.

To get your salary set up, visit Intuit Online Payroll by **clicking here.** To make it even easier for you, I've even included screenshots of the entire setup process below, along with some comments and further explanation for many of the questions.

I realize a lot of these questions are self-explanatory, so I would recommend that you go through them yourself and just refer back to this section if you have any questions.

Here's what you're going to see after clicking the link above (you may need to scroll down the page to view this section that gives you the free trial option):

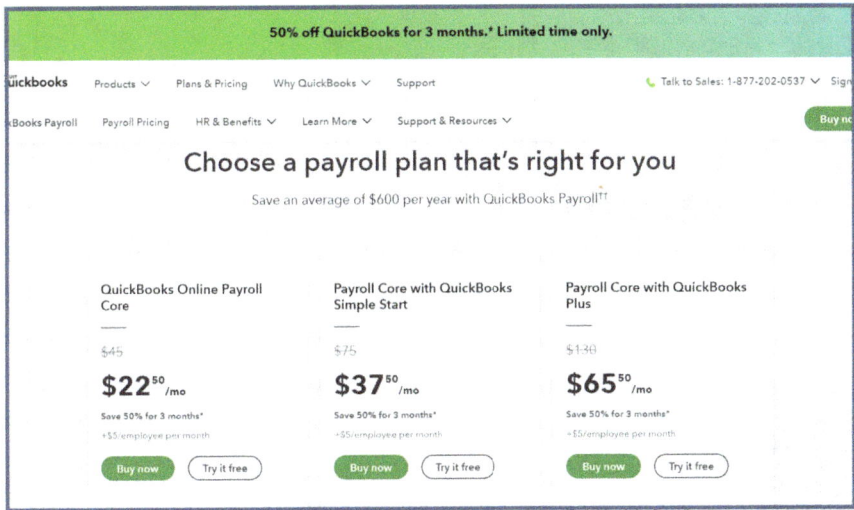

You really only need the first option for $22/mo unless you want to try out QuickBooks to handle your income and expense tracking, which is outside of the scope of this ebook. Once you click the "Try it free" button, it'll prompt you to create a new account and enter your payment info. Note that the free trial is for 30 days, then charges you a promotional rate of $22/mo for the next 3 months, then it goes up to $45/mo. This is a really good deal since it includes all your payroll tax reports. Hiring someone to run payroll every month and file quarterly reports would run you at least $100-150/mo.

Link: https://quickbooks.intuit.com/payroll/core/

49

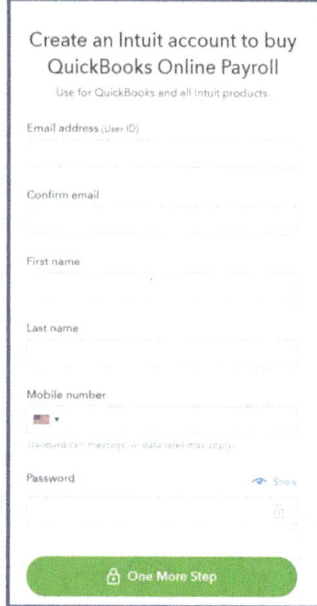

Create an Intuit account to buy QuickBooks Online Payroll

Use for QuickBooks and all Intuit products.

Email address (User ID)

Confirm email

First name

Last name

Mobile number

🇺🇸 ▾

Standard call, message, or data rates may apply.

Password   👁 Show

🔒 One More Step

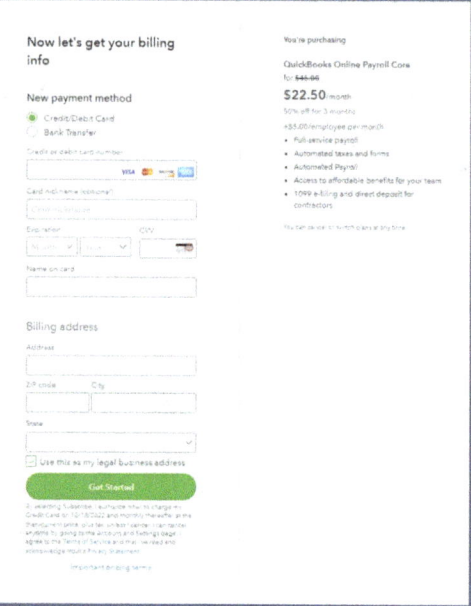

Now let's get your billing info

New payment method

⦿ Credit/Debit Card
◯ Bank Transfer

Credit or debit card number

VISA · mastercard · DISCOVER · AMEX

Card nickname (optional)

Expiration   CVV

Name on card

Billing address

Address

ZIP code   City

State

☐ Use this as my legal business address

Get Started

By selecting Subscribe, I authorize Intuit to charge my Credit Card on 12/18/2022 and monthly thereafter at the then-current price until I cancel. I can cancel anytime by going to the Account and Settings page. I agree to the Terms of Service and the revised and acknowledge Intuit's Privacy Statement.

Important pricing terms

You're purchasing

QuickBooks Online Payroll Core
for $45.00

$22.50/month

50% off for 3 months

+$5.00/employee per month

- Full-service payroll
- Automated taxes and forms
- Automated Payroll
- Access to affordable benefits for your team
- 1099 e-filing and direct deposit for contractors

You can cancel or switch plans at any time

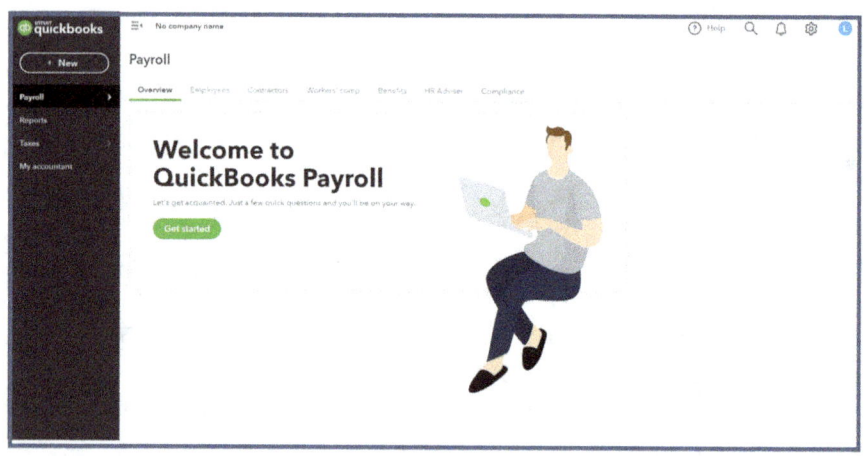

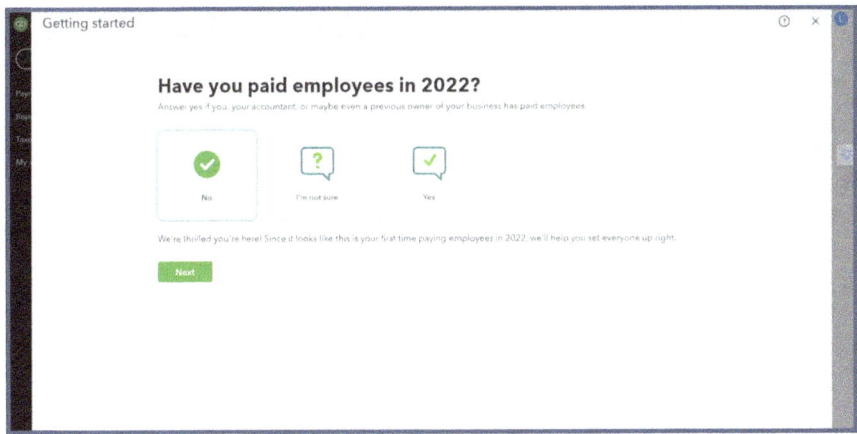

Since it's going to be a week or so before you get your LLC docs from the SOS, get your bank account setup and start depositing money into it, I would select the first of next month as your next payday, especially if you're close to the end of a quarter, then you'll avoid having to file a quarterly payroll tax return for only one payday.

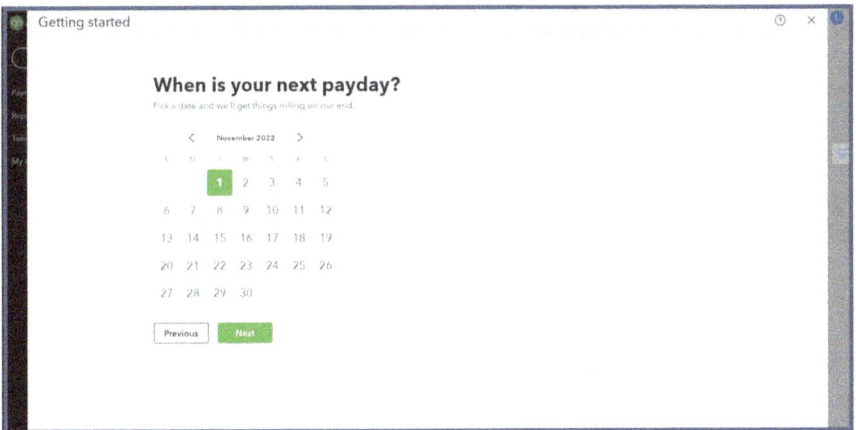

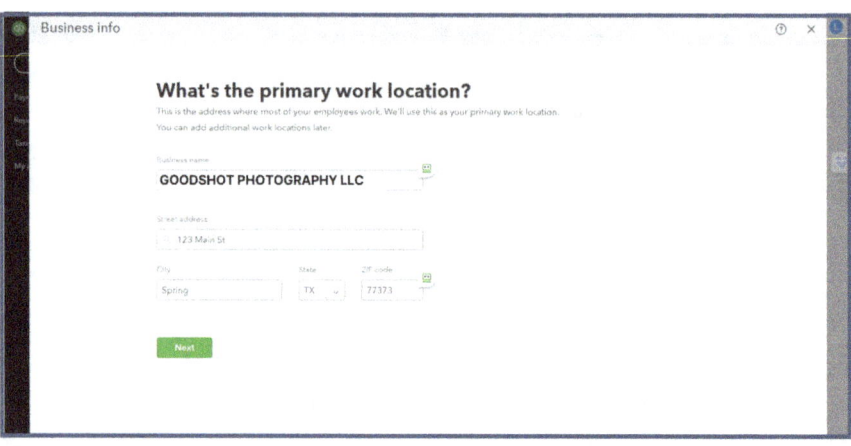

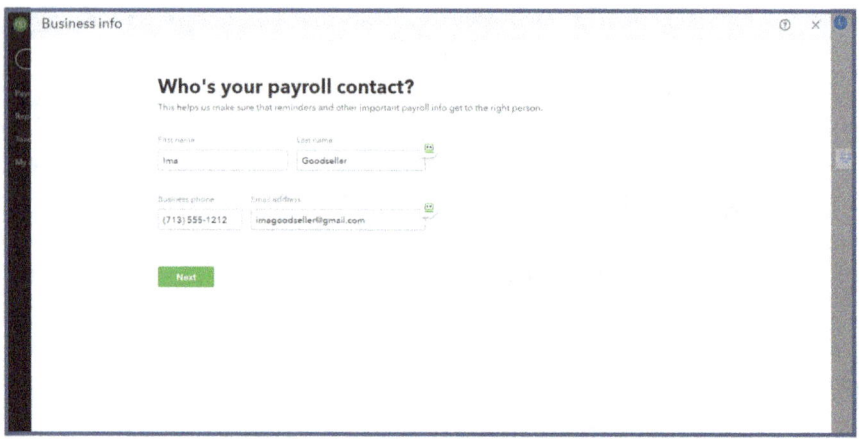

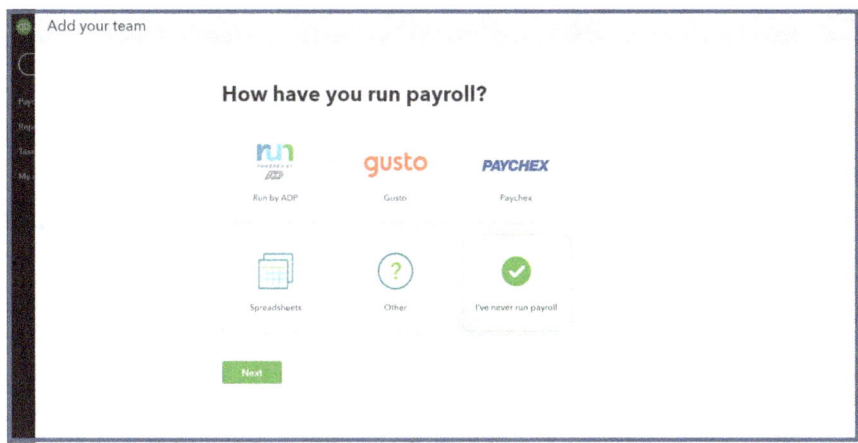

Here's where you'll add yourself as an employee. Once you do, you'll receive an email from your new employer (your LLC) asking you to set up your employee info for direct deposit, as well as your SSN, withholding, etc.

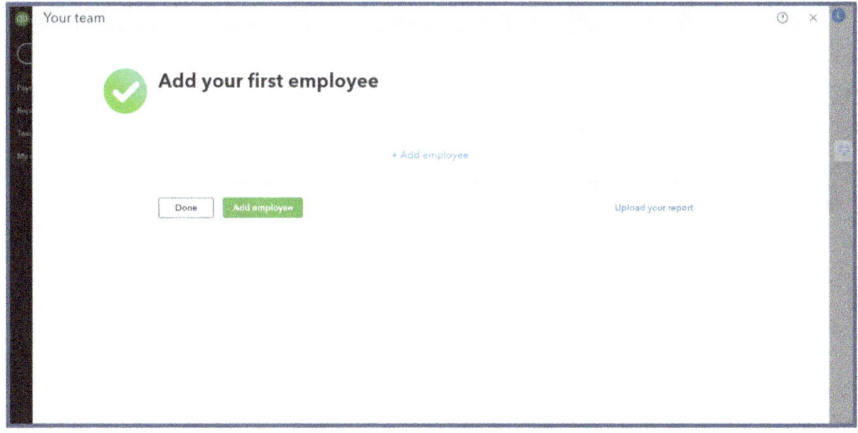

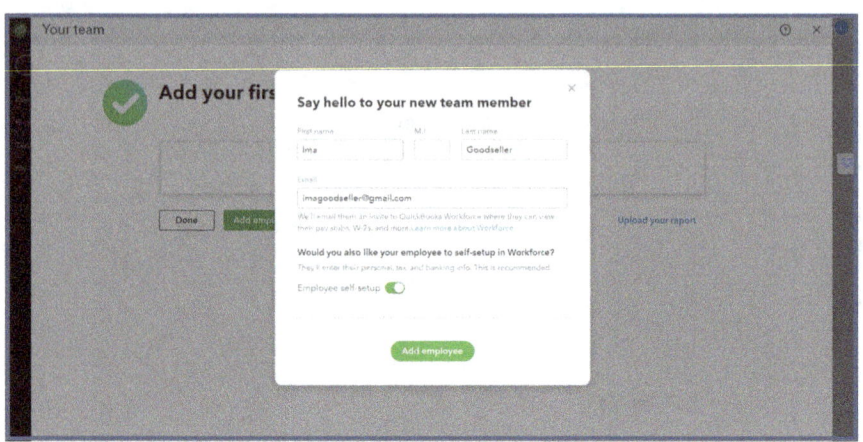

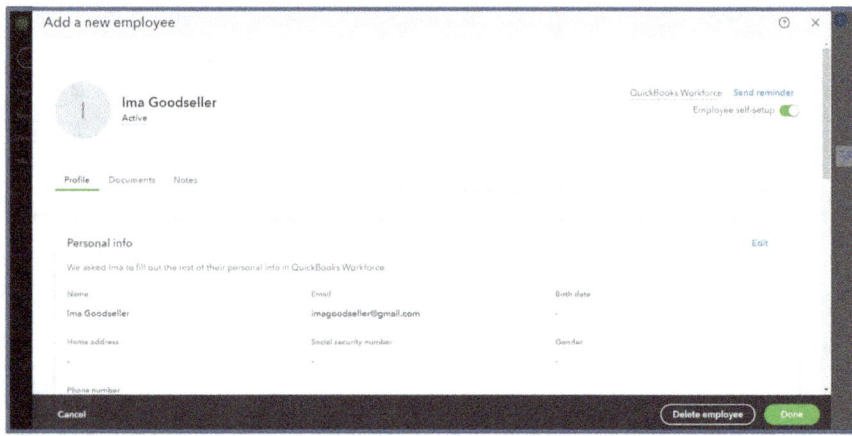

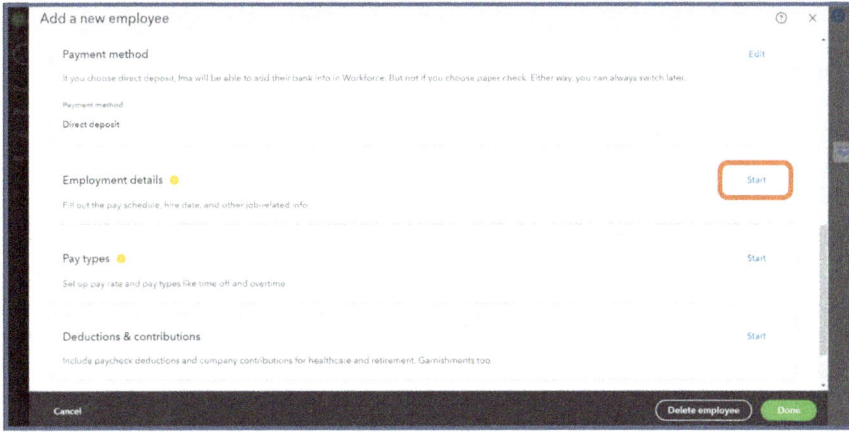

Once you enter your info as a new employee, click on the blue "Start" link to the right of "Employment Details" to get to the following screen. Here you'll enter the same date for Hire Date as you did for Next Payday earlier. Then click in the dropdown for Pay Schedule and select "Add Pay Schedule".

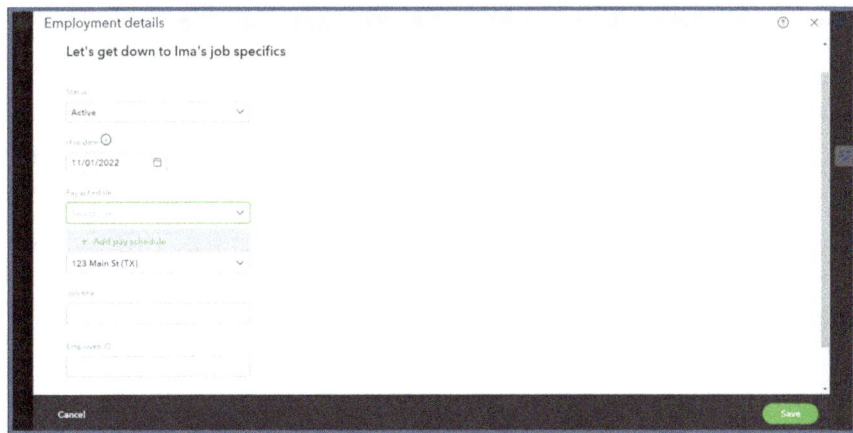

For the Pay Frequency, you can select "Every month" or if you want to pay yourself more frequently, you're obviously welcome to, I've just found it easier if you can set it up for once a month or even on the 1st and 15th. But if you do want to pay yourself more frequently, you won't get charged any extra by Intuit for doing so.

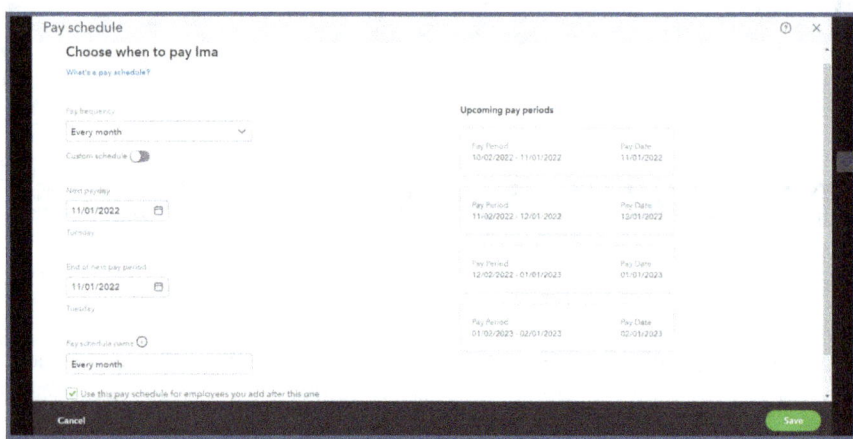

Now select how much you want to pay yourself. Again, you can refer to the Quick and Easy Cash Flow Plan in Appendix A to calculate what your salary should be. You can leave all of the other payment types alone. Hit "Save" and return to the dashboard.

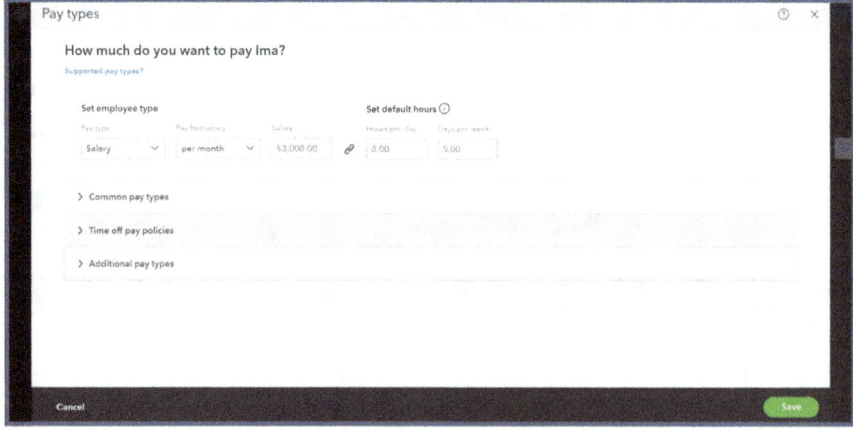

Until your LLC establishes a 401(k) or another company-sponsored retirement account, you can skip that section. Next up are some questions about paying payroll taxes and filing all the necessary reports, so go ahead and click the "Start" button next to "Fill in your tax info".

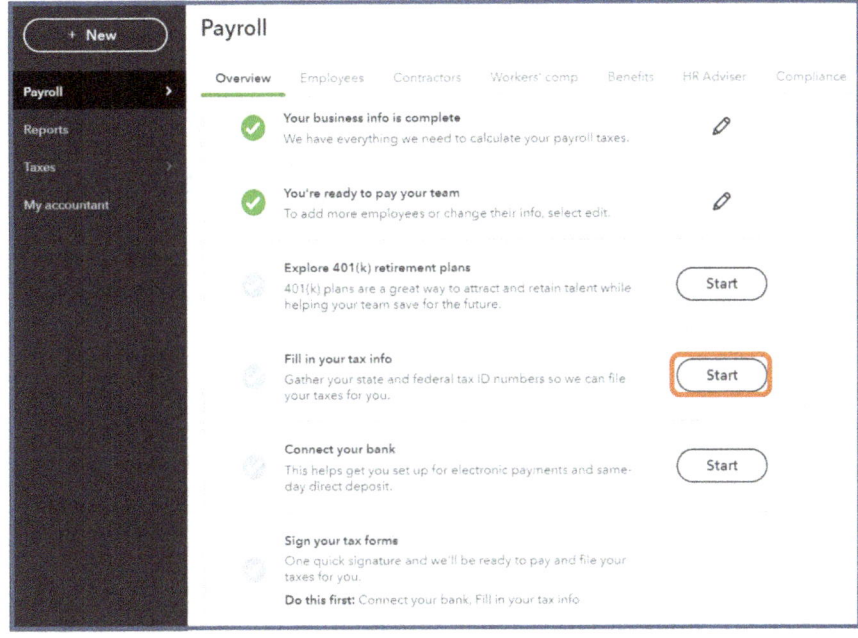

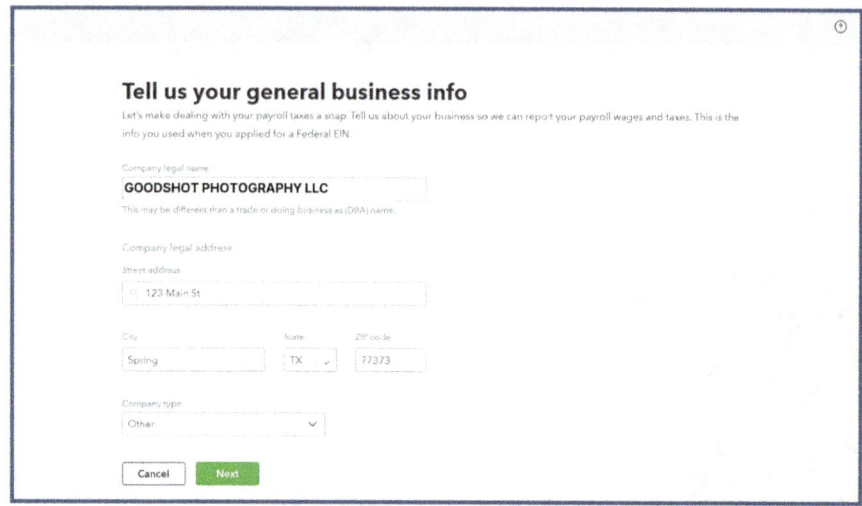

Tell us your general business info

Let's make dealing with your payroll taxes a snap. Tell us about your business so we can report your payroll wages and taxes. This is the info you used when you applied for a Federal EIN.

Company legal name

GOODSHOT PHOTOGRAPHY LLC

This may be different than a trade or doing business as (DBA) name.

Company legal address

Street address

🏠 123 Main St

City | State | ZIP code
Spring | TX ⌄ | 77373

Company type

Other ⌄

Cancel   Next

Enter your EIN and select that you'll be filing Form 941. The rule here is that if your federal payroll tax liability is less than $2,500 for the quarter, you can pay these taxes quarterly. If it exceeds $2,500, you're required to pay monthly. Assuming you're the only employee of your new LLC (or maybe it's just you and your spouse), and assuming that you're paying yourself a "reasonable" modest salary of around $24,000 or less each, you should fall under the quarterly filing requirements.

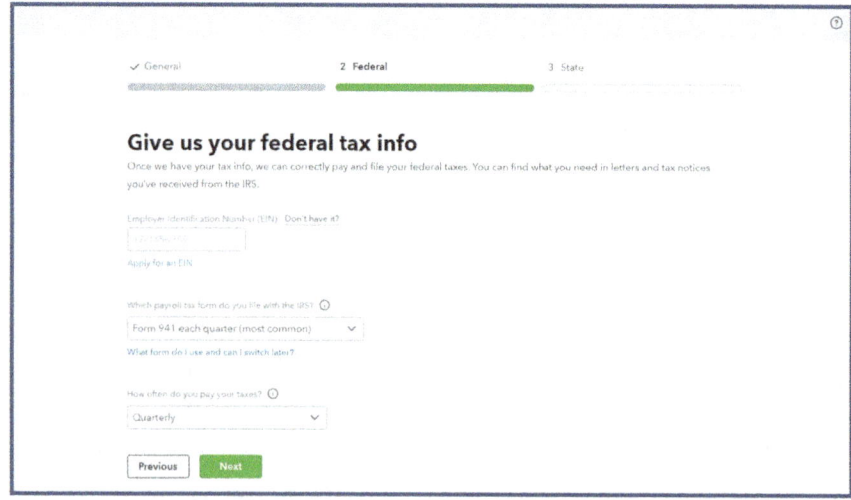

✓ General   2 **Federal**   3 State

Give us your federal tax info

Once we have your tax info, we can correctly pay and file your federal taxes. You can find what you need in letters and tax notices you've received from the IRS.

Employer Identification Number (EIN) Don't have it?

Apply for an EIN

Which payroll tax form do you file with the IRS? ⓘ

Form 941 each quarter (most common) ⌄

What form do I use and can I switch later?

How often do you pay your taxes? ⓘ

Quarterly ⌄

Previous   Next

As of the date of this publication, Intuit Online Payroll doesn't register your business with any of the state workforce agencies, so you'll have to do that part yourself. But once you've registered with the state and you get your state taxpayer number, Intuit will allow you to file and pay both the federal and state agencies electronically.

Each state is different when it comes to state income taxes, unemployment taxes, etc. In this example, Texas doesn't impose a state income tax on individuals but does have state unemployment tax that's required to be paid by all employers. If you're located in Texas, you'll need to click here to go to the Texas Workforce Commission (TWC) website. Once you've registered, make sure you print or save the "Registration Summary" page before closing your browser, as this will have your new TWC account number on it, which you'll enter below. If you're in another state, Intuit has a handy page with links to all of the state employment tax agencies here. Then, come on back over here and pick up where you left off. Or you can finish the Intuit payroll setup without your state tax information, and just log back in after you finish registering with your state employment tax agency and enter your info then. Either way, your call.

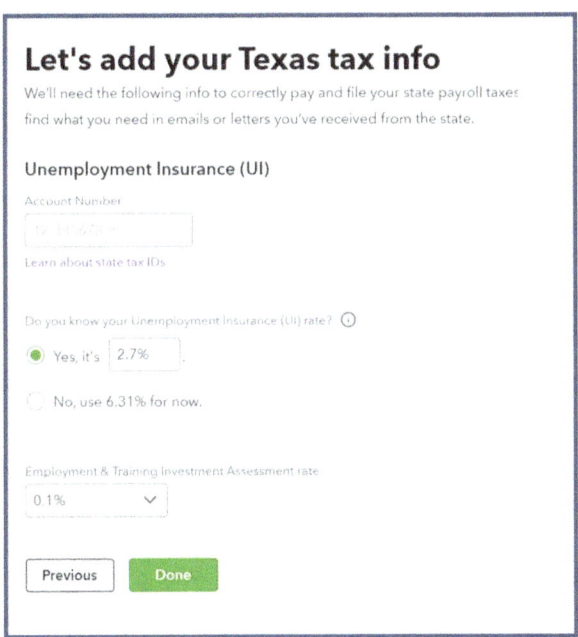

Even if you haven't yet received your new employer packet from TWC, you can go ahead and answer "Yes" for the question above. For all new businesses in Texas, the rate is always 2.7% of the first $9,000 of wages paid to each employee. So your new LLC will only pay $243 per year if you're the only employee. Part of your tax rate is what's called an Employment & Training Investment Assessment of 0.1% which is supposedly deposited into some employment and training investment holding fund, likely never to be seen again. Maybe that's really the state's "let's have an annual block party with the IRS guys" fund, who knows?

That's pretty much it for this step. Your salary is all set up, just remember to come back to this part if you didn't get to enter your state employment tax account number and rate yet. Next, click the start button next to "Connect to your bank".

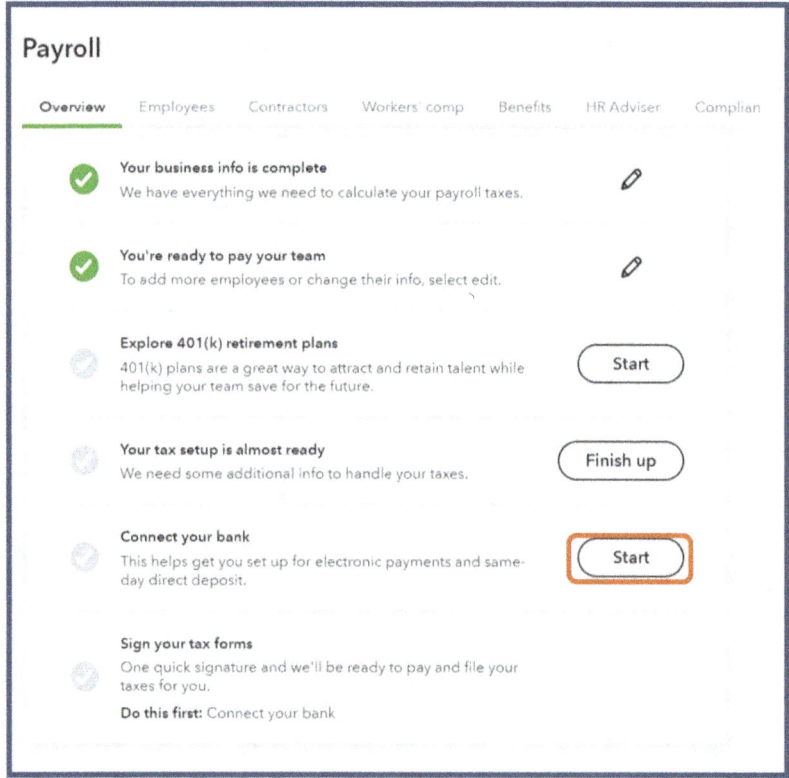

If you're still waiting for your LLC package from the SOS, then you'll need to come back to this section later once you have your new LLC bank account setup. Otherwise, go ahead and go through the steps to set up your direct deposit and electronic filing options for your payroll taxes. I won't bore you with a bunch of screenshots because it's pretty self-explanatory, just contact info for your business, you as the "principal officer" of the company" and your business bank info.

Once you complete that section, click the start button next to "Sign your tax forms".

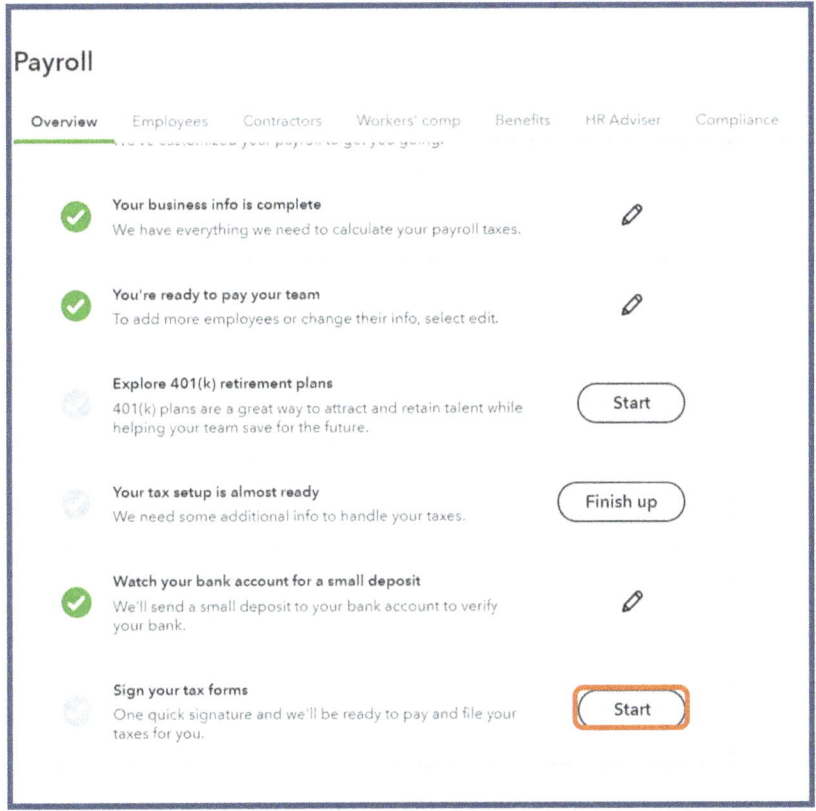

My personal opinion: letting QuickBooks file and pay everything automatically is the way to go. I promise you, it makes this whole payroll thing so much easier to manage.

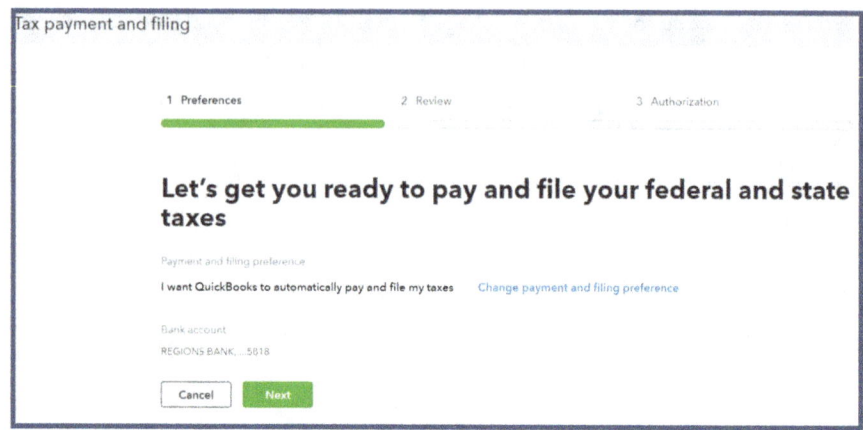

The next few pages are just to review your information and electronically sign authorizing them to file your payroll tax forms on your behalf.

After this initial enrollment is completed, all you have to do is login every pay period and tell Intuit to pay your salary, and it will be direct deposited to your account just like magic!

Next up, we'll cover the second way you'll want to pay yourself from the LLC, the part that will be excluded from the 15.3% self-employment tax. So let's keep on rollin'!

Step 5:
Lease Your Vehicle to Your LLC

As a business owner now, another way to take money out of your business without it being subject to the 15% self-employment tax is to have your company pay you a monthly lease payment for the business use of your vehicle. Your LLC will deduct the lease payment as a business expense, but on the flip side, you have to pick it up as rental income on your personal tax return, but now it's considered passive income that's not subject to the 15% self-employment tax.

Call around some local dealerships to find out how much it would cost you to lease a vehicle similar to yours, and use that as a guide for how much your LLC should pay you to lease your vehicle from you.

I've even included a standard Automobile Lease Agreement in Appendix C for you to fill out based on what amount you decide. Keep this agreement with your other LLC files as proof that you have a legitimate lease agreement between yourself and your company.

What you'll do is simply continue to pay your car payment out of your personal account, but start paying for all of your vehicle operating expenses such as car maintenance, insurance, fuel & oil changes out of your business account. It's the same as if your LLC were to go out and lease a vehicle from a third party. The LLC would pay them a monthly lease, and it would also be required to pay for the insurance, fuel, maintenance, etc.

Next up, reimburse yourself for something you're already paying for anyway!

Step 6: Reimburse Yourself for Your Home Office

Another advantage of your LLC being taxed as an S-Corporation (that's what you did when you filed Form 2553) is that a corporation can reimburse its employees for their home office expenses without the employee claiming the reimbursement as income. So your LLC gets to write off your home office, and even though it's paying you, it falls under the reimbursement rules that say that those payments are not taxable to you as the employee when you receive them.

This is just one more way to take money out of the LLC that's not only exempt from the self-employment tax, but exempt from any taxes at all. Now that's my kind of write-off!

Now the IRS does set some guidelines for you to be able to claim the home office. These are called the "Convenience-of-Employer Test", and generally you must:
1. Use the office for administrative or management activities (this would include checking business emails, paying your business bills, strategic planning, etc)
2. Have no other fixed place where you conduct substantial administrative or management activities (by the way, the broker's office where you go every day doesn't constitute an administrative office if you use it primarily as a place to "meet and greet" clients, whether on the phone or in person)
3. Use the office exclusively and regularly as a place of business (even if it's only used for your administrative office)

In other words, to take advantage of the home office deduction, you'll want to use your home office as your "primary administrative" office, and your firm's office as your "meet and greet" or sales office.

All you need to do is figure out how much of your household expenses should be allocated to your home office, by filling out a Form 8829 (see link below) as a worksheet. (By the way, you don't need to file this form with the IRS, just use it as a guide to calculate how much your LLC needs to reimburse you each month). Then write a check out of your LLC bank account once a month, payable to you for that amount.

Download Form 8829 by **clicking here.**

You'll notice that Form 8829 has two columns, one for direct expenses and one for indirect expenses. The majority of your expenses are going to fall into the indirect column, if they are expenses for the whole house, such as utilities, mortgage interest, etc. However, if you perform any kind of repairs or maintenance solely on the area you're claiming as your home office, such as painting that area or installing a new ceiling fan in that room, that would go in the direct expense column.

Easy enough, isn't it? Alright, you're almost finished, so let's keep moving...

Link: https://www.irs.gov/pub/irs-pdf/f8829.pdf

Step 7:
Set Aside Money For Taxes

Okay, now it's time to figure out how much money to set aside for your taxes. I know, you don't like thinking about that part, none of us do, but it's a whole lot better than being surprised and unprepared at the end of the year, right? Plus, you can feel better knowing that you're going to be paying a lot less tax than you would if you didn't follow this system.

Each month you should be setting aside a portion of your income to pay both your quarterly payroll taxes (the taxes that should be withheld from each of your paychecks) and your estimated income taxes (the taxes on all of your other income).

PAYROLL TAX
Remember that your payroll taxes are the taxes that are being withheld from your paycheck each month along with the LLC's share of the payroll tax. If you set up your salary according to my recommendations in Step 4 above, Intuit will electronically pay these taxes to the IRS on your behalf each time it pays your salary.

ESTIMATED TAXES
Your estimated taxes, on the other hand, are the taxes you're paying on all of your other income besides your salary, and should be paid out of your personal bank account. A good general rule of thumb for your estimated taxes is to set aside roughly 15% of your sales for the month and put it into a separate "Tax Savings Account". These estimated payments are due April 15th, June 15th, September 15th, and the last one on January 15th. Use IRS Form 1040 ES when making each of these payments. You can download this form by **clicking here.**

Link: https://www.irs.gov/pub/irs-pdf/f8829.pdf

Step 8:
Pay Yourself A
Tax-Free Dividend

Alright, so now that we've paid all of these things with pre-tax dollars, I bet you're wondering what to do with the rest of the money that's in your bank account at the end of each month. The other nice thing about having an LLC that's taxed as an S-Corporation is that you don't get hit with the so-called "double taxation" that you may have heard about with a regular C-Corp.

According to the IRS, as long as you're paying yourself a "reasonable salary" and a "reasonable lease", then you're allowed to also pay yourself a tax-free dividend. Dividends paid out of an S-Corp (or an LLC taxed as an S-Corp) are not considered a tax deductible expense for the LLC, but rather a return of capital, which is not taxable to you when you receive it, making it essentially tax free (or really "tax neutral", although "tax free" has a much nicer ring to it).

The dividend can be any amount you need to cover the rest of your personal expenses, and it can be paid at any time. The main thing is to make sure they are reasonable compared to your salary and lease payment. In other words, you don't want to pay yourself a $12,000 a year salary and $75,000 a year in dividends.

However, there is one caveat with the dividends. If your LLC has more than one member, you're required to pay each member the same amount in dividends for the year. This is one of the restrictions of having your LLC taxed as an S-Corporation.

From my experience with the IRS, if your dividends are higher than your salary by around 25-35%, they may reclassify your dividends as salary and make you pay the additional 15% tax on it, plus any penalties and interest. So be sure to use my Quick and Easy Cash Flow Plan in Appendix A to figure out what amounts to pay yourself.

Step 9:
Plan Your Next Vacation

So you've set up your LLC, you've done everything necessary to make sure you get the best tax treatment, you've started paying yourself a salary, rent, and a tax-free dividend. Whew! Now that wasn't so bad, was it?

The next and last step is to plan your next vacation. This is my favorite part because as a business owner, at least once a year you should have a business meeting to discuss things like how much money you made last year, how much money you're going to make next year, and any changes you want to make in the way you operate your business. Well, guess what? You can write off those meeting expenses as a tax-deductible business expense. And guess where a lot of businesses have those annual meetings? Places like Las Vegas, a ski resort in Breckenridge, or maybe on a cruise ship to the Caribbean!

Now if you have kids and you take them to Disney, you might have a hard time convincing an IRS agent that it was all business related, so you might just take a portion of the expenses for that trip.

So get started planning that next vacation, I mean "annual business meeting".

Step 10:
Bonus Tip to Avoid Underpayment Penalty

If you're setting up your LLC late in the year and are worried that maybe you haven't paid in enough taxes during the year, I have a sneaky, but 100% legal trick for avoiding getting hit with an underpayment penalty.

What's an underpayment penalty, you ask? Well, if you were a "normal" W-2 employee working for a company, your employer would take payroll taxes out of each of your paychecks and pay them to the IRS throughout the year. But since you're self- employed, you're not paying taxes throughout the year by way of payroll deductions, so the IRS wants you to pay Estimated Taxes every quarter based on the total tax you owed for the prior year. You know, they want your money as soon as possible so they can start spending it on things like hiring 87,000 more IRS agents to audit more of us hard-working Americans. (Don't get me started...)

This is where the underpayment penalty comes in. If you don't pay those estimated payments during the year, if you end up owing money at tax time, you will get slammed with a 6% penalty on the amount that you owed but didn't get paid throughout the year.

Well, there's a little IRS loophole that says that payroll taxes get treated as if they were paid evenly throughout the year, even if there's a large lump sum payment that gets paid once at the end of the year. Now there's a caveat, this doesn't mean you don't have to pay any of your payroll taxes until the end of the year, but it does mean that if you didn't pay your estimated taxes while you were self-employed (before starting your LLC), you could pay yourself a large paycheck (say $20,000) at the end of the year and withhold a large portion of it in Federal Withholding (say $18,000) and the IRS would treat it as having been paid throughout the year and would not charge you with the underpayment penalty.

So for example:

For tax year 2021, let's say you ended up with a $20,000 total tax liability (that would be line 24 on your Form 1040), so the IRS would have required you to pay at least 100% of that amount in 2022 estimated quarterly tax payments. Well, let's say you didn't realize that was even a rule or maybe you just didn't have money during the year because business was a little slow the first half of the year, but then business picked up a lot in the second half, whatever the reason.

Well, now that you're a new employee of the LLC, you can pay yourself a large paycheck at the end of the year and withhold most of it in federal income taxes (FIT) so your net paycheck is very little or even zero. In doing so, all of that FIT withholding should cover any unpaid estimated payments and be treated by the IRS as if you had paid those during the year, thus avoiding the 6% underpayment penalty. YOU'RE WELCOME!

I hope that all makes sense. And if you're still not 100% sure exactly how much you should pay yourself or have other questions related to this strategy, you can always hire a CPA to help you with some year-end tax planning. They'll be able to look at your overall tax situation to provide the best advice, since the ebook is really only meant to cover this one specific area of your financial planning.

Recap of Filing Requirements

Here's a recap of the filing requirements you'll need to keep up with each year.

Payroll Reports:

If you followed my advice above and signed up for the Intuit Payroll Service, they will handle preparing and filing all of the payroll tax reports for you, so it makes all of this easy as pie. But just so you know...

IRS Form 941 is where you report how much FICA and Federal Income Tax (FIT) you withheld from your salary for the quarter, plus the portion of taxes that your LLC matches. This must be filed with the IRS by the last day of the month following each quarter, so the due dates are as follows:

1st Quarter (Jan – Mar) due April 30th
2nd Quarter (Apr – June) due July 31st
3rd Quarter (July – Sept) due October 31st
4th Quarter (Oct – Dec) due January 31st

Depending on the state you live in, you may also have quarterly state payroll tax reports that you will need to file. The due dates for the state reports are typically on the same schedule as that for the federal reports.

There's also an IRS Form 940 that's due by January 31st that reports your federal unemployment tax for the year. This would also be prepared and filed by Intuit if you signed up for their service.

As an employee of your LLC, you'll also need to file a W-2 and W-3 with the Social Security Administration before February 28th. Again, Intuit would handle these, too.

Income Tax Returns:

As an LLC that's taxable as an S-corp, you're required to file Form 1120S with the IRS each year by March 15th. Although the LLC pays no federal income tax (not to be confused with the payroll tax on your salary), it still has to file the 1120S each year. As part of preparing the 1120S, a Form K-1 is also prepared and given to each of the owners of the LLC showing their portion of the net income, which in turn gets reported on your personal tax return (Form 1040). That's where you pay the tax on the net business income.

As for the state compliance, most states require that you file some form of a state LLC tax return also, or at least pay an annual fee to maintain it. Because each state is different, it's difficult to cover the rules for all 50 states, so you'll want to check out the state revenue department where you live. For Texas, there's a Franchise Tax Report that's required to be filed every May 15th starting the year after you incorporate, but if your sales are under $1M for the year, there's no tax due, but you still have to file a "No Tax Due Information Report" (form 05-163), and a "Public Information Report" (form 05-102) to maintain your charter with the state. These are both fairly simple, one-page forms and can be found on the Texas Comptroller's website here.

One key thing to remember when it comes to your state filing requirement is this: if you don't keep up with the annual compliance with the state (the very agency that is giving you permission to do business within a separate legal structure), they can revoke your status as an LLC which will expose you to all of the legal liability and tax implications of operating as a sole proprietor again. So **MAKE SURE YOU STAY COMPLIANT WITH YOUR STATE...ON TIME...EVERY YEAR!!!** (Ok, that's all I'm going to say about that, so I hope you get how critical this is.)

Final Thoughts

You made it!! I want to thank you for purchasing and reading this ebook. I realize that this all may seem like a lot to do, but it's definitely worth a few short hours' worth of work in exchange for hundreds of thousands of dollars in tax savings over the life of your career. On top of the tax savings, I know it will provide you with some peace of mind knowing that you're taking control of your taxes.

And if you've read through all of this and you're not sure if you have the time or patience to set all of this up yourself, PLEASE don't let the IRS rob you of your hard-earned money by not implementing this system. We'll be more than happy to refer you to someone who can put all of this in place for you. Even with the fees you might pay a CPA or attorney to set all this up for you, you'll still be saving thousands of dollars each and every year.

If this is something you'd like more information on, please send us an email at info@manifestgroup.biz with your name and contact information and we'll make sure you don't lose out on any of these amazing tax savings.

The main thing is, I want to see you take action and commit to keeping as many of those dollars where they belong, IN YOUR POCKETS, not the coffers of the IRS!

Appendix A

Quick and Easy Cash Flow Plan

Step 1: Estimate your average monthly net income

A. Total sales you expect to earn over the next 12 months: $ _____

B. Divide line A by 12 *(this is your average monthly commission)*: $ _____

C. Monthly business expenses*(exclude salary & lease, but go ahead* $ _____
    and include car gas & car insurance):

D. Monthly vehicle lease payment *(based on similar lease rates):* $ _____

E. Monthly home office reimbursement *(based on Form 8829):* $ _____

Subtract C, D, & E from B above *(this is your Net Income) :* $ _____

Step 2: Split monthly net income into Savings, Salary and Dividends

Monthly savings for estimated taxes
(15-20% of commissions is a good rule): $ _____

Monthly Salary	Member 1:	$ _____
(this is what gets hit with the additional 15.3% tax)		
	Member 2:	$ _____
Monthly Dividend	Member 1:	$ _____
(**must** be same amount to each member):		
	Member 2:	$ _____

Note: Obviously, you're going to have some good months and some bad ones, so the amounts for salaries and dividends can fluctuate up or down each month as needed, but try to keep the monthly lease payment the same, since you now have a formal lease agreement in place. This helps to build your case if the IRS ever decides to look at you.

Appendix B

FREELANCER TAX SAVINGS: 5-YEAR PROJECTION
Schedule C versus LLC

Assumptions:	Year 1	Year 2	Year 3	Year 4	Year 5
Average Monthly Sales:	$ 8,000	$ 10,000	$ 12,000	$ 15,000	$ 20,000
Average Monthly Expenses:	$ 1,800	$ 2,000	$ 2,500	$ 3,000	$ 4,000
Annual Salary Paid to You from LLC:	$ 18,000	$ 26,000	$ 28,000	$ 36,000	$ 48,000

Tax Impact of Filing Schedule C (self-employed)

Reported on 1040:					
Annual Net Income (Gets reported on Sch. C of 1040)	$ 74,400	$ 96,000	$ 114,000	$ 144,000	$ 192,000
Less Standard Deduction	$ (12,950)	$ (12,950)	$ (12,950)	$ (12,950)	$ (12,950)
Less Deduction for 1/2 of SE Tax	$ (5,256)	$ (6,782)	$ (8,054)	$ (10,173)	$ (11,685)
Taxable Income	$ 56,194	$ 76,268	$ 92,996	$ 120,877	$ 167,365
Federal Tax*	$ 7,979	$ 10,592	$ 11,103	$ 14,324	$ 20,990
Self-employment Tax	$ 10,512	$ 13,564	$ 16,108	$ 20,347	$ 23,370
Total Income Tax Liability	$ 18,492	$ 24,157	$ 27,211	$ 34,670	$ 44,360

Tax Impact of Filing LLC

Reported on LLC					
Sales minus Expenses	$ 74,400	$ 96,000	$ 114,000	$ 144,000	$ 192,000
Less Salary Paid to Owner	$ (18,000)	$ (26,000)	$ (28,000)	$ (36,000)	$ (48,000)
Payroll Tax Expense (Federal only)	$ (1,377)	$ (1,989)	$ (2,142)	$ (2,754)	$ (3,672)
Net Business Income (This amount flows to your 1040)	$ 55,023	$ 68,011	$ 83,858	$ 105,246	$ 140,328
Reported on 1040					
Salary from LLC	$ 18,000	$ 26,000	$ 28,000	$ 36,000	$ 48,000
Net Income from LLC (Gets reported on Sch. E of 1040)	$ 55,023	$ 68,011	$ 83,858	$ 105,246	$ 140,328
Less Standard Deduction	$ (12,950)	$ (12,950)	$ (12,950)	$ (12,950)	$ (12,950)
Taxable Income	$ 60,073	$ 81,061	$ 98,908	$ 128,296	$ 175,378
Federal Tax*	$ 8,833	$ 11,503	$ 12,087	$ 15,435	$ 22,549
FICA Tax Withheld from Salary	$ 1,377	$ 1,989	$ 2,142	$ 2,754	$ 3,672
Total Income Tax Liability	$ 10,210	$ 13,492	$ 14,229	$ 18,189	$ 26,221

TOTAL TAX SAVINGS BY FILING LLC RATHER THAN SCH. C:	$ 8,282	$ 10,665	$ 12,982	$ 16,481	$ 18,139

Other costs associated with maintaining your LLC					
Cost of this e-book	$ 27				
Initial Setup of LLC	$ 325				
Preparation of LLC & Personal Tax Return	$ 650	$ 650	$ 650	$ 650	$ 650
Intuit Payroll service (@ $50/mo)	$ 600	$ 600	$ 600	$ 600	$ 600
Tax savings on the above costs (the LLC gets to write them off)	$ (401)	$ (313)	$ (313)	$ (313)	$ (313)
Net Annual Cost to Maintain LLC	$ 1,202	$ 938	$ 938	$ 938	$ 938

ACTUAL DOLLARS THAT YOU PUT BACK INTO YOUR POCKET BY USING "THE FREELANCER'S LLC PLAYBOOK"	$ 7,080	$ 9,727	$12,045	$15,543	$17,202

*Note: Federal tax calculations are based on 2022 tax rates for the Single Filing Status, and on the assumption that tax rates will remain the same over the next 5 years. Also note that no provision has been made for state income taxes, as they vary from state to state.

Appendix C

SAMPLE AUTOMOBILE LEASE

This automobile lease ("Lease") is made this the _____ day of , 20____ between
_____ (hereafter referred to as "Lessor", having his principal
place of business at _____ (address) and
_____ ("Lessee"). Lessor and Lessee hereby agree as follows:

1. Lessor hereby leases to the Lessee, for a term of _____ months the following
described automobile: (Make, Model, Year, VIN). The term and rent shall commence on the
_____ day of _____, 20___, and end on the ____ day of _____, 20___.

2. Lessee will acquire license plates registered in his name under the laws of the state of
_____.

3. Lessee will maintain, or cause to be maintained, the automobile in good working
condition. Nothing in this agreement shall require Lessor to provide or pay for, or cause to
be provided or paid for, any gasoline, oil, antifreeze, washing or storage for the automobile.

4. Lessor will reimburse Lessee for the cost of any inspection of the automobile as required
by laws of the state of _____.

5. Lessee agrees to pay to Lessor at _____
(address) the sum of $_____, as rent, on the first day of each and every calendar
month. The rent for the first and last month of the term, unless the term starts on the first
day of the month and ends on the first day of the month, shall be apportioned on the basis
which the number of days of the term in the month bears to the whole number of days in
such month.

6. The automobile leased under this agreement will be used and operated in a careful
manner and Lessee will pay or cause to be paid any fines imposed by any governmental
authority levied upon the automobile and/or its driver as the result of any act or omission
during the term the automobile is leased under this agreement.

7. Lessee will not use or allow the automobile to be used for any illegal purpose and will
reimburse Lessor if the automobile is confiscated and for expenses incurred as a result of
any confiscation or attempted confiscation by any governmental authority whatsoever,
whenever such confiscation and expenses, or either, is caused by the illegal use of such
automobile while the automobile is leased under this agreement.

8. Lessee will keep and maintain the automobile in good running order and will see that it
stays in good repair and is properly serviced at the expense of Lessee.

9. Immediately on the discovery of the need of any repair or servicing of the automobile,
Lessee shall cause such automobile to be taken to an authorized service station of the
manufacturer of such automobile. The cost of such repair may be deducted by the Lessee
from the next rental payment due Lessor under this agreement, provided Lessee shall
make no repairs the cost of which shall exceed $_____ without the written consent
of Lessor first obtained.

At the time of making such deduction, Lessee shall provide Lessor with an itemized invoice evidencing payment for the repairs for which such deduction is claimed. Notwithstanding the foregoing, Lessee is responsible for payment for repairs resulting from the negligence of Lessee or anyone driving the car with or without the consent of Lessee, or the violation by Lessee of the terms of this agreement, and no such deduction from rental payments may be made.

10. The automobile will be kept and maintained in a garage or other covered storage space except when in use.

11. Lessee at his/her expense will pay for, at his sole expense, all gasoline, oil, antifreeze, washing, and storage fees for the automobile leased under this agreement.

12. Lessee will acquire, pay for, and maintain automobile indemnity insurance, including public liability and property damage insurance, issued by a responsible company or companies, protecting the interests of both Lessee and Lessor against liability for damage, personal injury or death caused by the automobile or the operation of the automobile to the extent of not less than $_____ per accident and not less than $_____ per person; and the sum of $_____ per accident against liability for damage to property caused by the operation of any automobile leased under this agreement, and Lessee agrees that the policy will include Lessor as a "named insured" and shall not be canceled until after _____ days notice to Lessor of intention to cancel, and the Lessee further agrees to furnish to Lessor prior, to the use or operation of any such automobile, a certificate of such insurance.

13. Should any claim be made or any action be commenced against Lessor arising from any of the causes covered by the insurance referred to in Paragraph 11, Lessor will promptly notify Lessee and Lessee will conduct the defense of any such claim or action at Lessee's expense, including all costs and attorneys' fees.

14. In the event of the cancellation of any public liability and property damage insurance required under the terms of this Lease, the use by Lessee of the automobile shall cease until all such insurance so canceled has been renewed or replaced.

15. Except as otherwise subsequently provided, upon the expiration of the term of this Lease or its earlier termination for any reason, the automobile shall be returned by Lessee to Lessor at (address).

16. If any default shall be made by Lessee in the payment when due, of any rent or other sum due under this agreement, or in the performance of any other provision, or if Lessee is or becomes unable to pay his/her debts from his/her own means as they become due, or if any receiver or trustee of the business or of the property or assets of the Lessee shall be appointed by any court, or if the Lessee shall abandon the automobiles, or if the Lessee shall otherwise, in any manner whatever, become unable to pay the rent specified here or to perform any of the provisions to be kept or performed by Lessee, then Lessor shall have the option, without notice to Lessee or demand for performance, to require Lessee to redeliver the automobile to Lessor at a location designated by Lessor at Lessee's expense.

17. Upon any such default, and with or without terminating or forfeiting this Lease and without in any way affecting any other right or remedy of Lessor or any duties or obligations of Lessee under this agreement, Lessor may lease the automobile as the agent and for the account of Lessee upon such terms and conditions as Lessor

advisable, in which event the rents received on any such lease shall be applied first to the expenses of leasing and collecting, including any necessary renovation or repairs, toward payment of all sums due or to become due to Lessor under this agreement, and if a sufficient sum shall not thus be realized to pay such rent and other charges, Lessee shall pay to Lessor monthly any deficiency.

18. Upon any such default, Lessor may terminate this Lease, in which event Lessee shall pay to Lessor the amount of rent that would have been paid to Lessor had there been no such default.

19. The foregoing remedies for default shall not be exclusive but shall be cumulative and in addition to all other remedies.

20. In case any litigation of any kind between Lessee and Lessor shall arise out of this Lease, and Lessor shall prevail in such litigation, Lessee agrees to pay Lessor a reasonable attorney's fee which shall be taxed by the court as part of the costs of such litigation.

21. Lessor will not be liable to Lessee for any loss of business or any other damage caused by any interruption of the service provided for here or otherwise.

22. Lessor does not assume any liability for any acts or omissions of Lessee or of any of Lessee's agents, employees or drivers and Lessee specifically releases Lessor from all such liability and agrees to indemnify and hold Lessor harmless of and from any and all such liability.

23. This is an automobile lease only, and the Lessee has acquired no right, title or interest in the automobile, except the right to use the same pursuant to the provisions of this Lease.

24. The term of this Lease shall be extended for an additional term of _____ months pursuant to the terms of this Lease, including this paragraph for renewal, unless either Lessor or Lessee, at least _____ days before the end of the term of this Lease, gives written notice to the other of intention to terminate this Lease on expiration of the term provided for in this agreement.

25. So long as the Lessee performs all of the terms and conditions of this Lease including payment of the rental, Lessee shall have the unrestricted lawful use of such automobile for any lawful purpose except the transportation of persons or property for hire.

26. Lessee will not assign or mortgage this Lease, or any interest in it, or permit the use of the automobile by any person other than Lessee or an adult member of his or her family or his or her agents or employees, nor sublet any automobile without the written consent of Lessor.

27. This lease agreement represents the entire agreement between the parties and no provision may be waived or modified, except by an instrument in writing signed by both of the parties.

WITNESS our signatures the day and year first written above.

Signature of Lessor_____ Signature of Lessee _____

Appendix D

Sample Operating Agreement of [Your Business Name], LLC
Limited Liability Company State of Texas

THIS OPERATING AGREEMENT is hereby established, this the [DAY] day of [MONTH], [YEAR], by [YOUR NAME], the Initial Member.

The Initial Member contemplates that additional Members may join the limited liability company in the future, and the following Operating Agreement has therefore been developed.

ARTICLE I
FORMATION OF LIMITED LIABILITY COMPANY

1. Formation of LLC. The Initial Member has formed a limited liability company in the State of Texas named [YOUR BUSINESS NAME], LLC ("LLC"). The operation of the LLC shall be governed by the terms of this Agreement and the applicable laws of the State of Texas relating to the formation, operation and taxation of an LLC. To the extent permitted by law, the terms and provisions of this Agreement shall control if there is a conflict between state law and this Agreement. The LLC elects to be taxed as a corporation.

2. Articles of Organization. The Initial Member has caused to be filed Articles of Organization, ("Articles") of record with the state, thereby creating the LLC.

3. Business. The business of the LLC shall be:

   a) To facilitate the purchase and sale of residential real estate as a licensed real estate agent.

         and

   b) To conduct or promote any lawful businesses or purposes that a limited liability company is legally allowed to conduct or promote, within this state or any other jurisdiction.

4. Registered Office and Registered Agent. The registered office and place of business of the LLC shall be [YOUR PHYSICAL ADDRESS] and the registered agent at such office shall be [YOUR NAME]. The registered office and/or registered agent may be changed from time to time.

5. Duration. The LLC will commence business as of the date of filing its Articles and will continue in perpetuity.

6. Fiscal Year. The LLC's fiscal and tax year shall end December 31.

ARTICLE II
MEMBERS

7. <u>Initial Member.</u> The Initial Member of the LLC is [YOUR NAME].

8. <u>Additional Members.</u> The first new Member, or new Members if several are to be added simultaneously, may be admitted only upon the approval of the Initial Member. Following the addition of a Member or Members, further new Members may be admitted only upon the consent of a majority of the existing Members and upon compliance with the provisions of this Agreement.

ARTICLE III
MANAGEMENT

9. <u>Management.</u> The Initial Member shall manage the LLC, and shall have authority to take all necessary and proper actions to conduct the business of the LLC. Anyone authorized by the Initial Member may take any authorized action on behalf of the LLC.

ARTICLE IV
CONTRIBUTIONS, PROFITS, LOSSES, AND DISTRIBUTIONS

10. <u>Interest of Members.</u> Each Member shall own a percentage interest (sometimes referred to as a share) in the LLC. The Member's percentage interest shall be based on the amount of cash or other property that the Member has contributed to the LLC and that percentage interest shall control the Member's share of the profits, losses, and distributions of the LLC.

11. <u>Initial Contribution.</u> The initial contribution of the Initial Member is $100.00, representing a 100% interest in the LLC.

12. <u>Additional Contributions.</u> In the event additional Members are added, upon a majority vote, the Members may be called upon to make additional cash contributions as may be necessary to carry on the LLC's business. The amount of any additional cash contribution shall be based on the Member's then existing percentage interest. To the extent a Member is unable to meet a cash call, the other Members can contribute the unmet call on a pro rata basis based on the Members' percentage interests at that time, and the percentage interest of each Member will be adjusted accordingly.

13. <u>Record of Contributions/Percentage Interests.</u> A record shall be kept of all contributions to, and percentage interests in, the LLC. This Agreement, any amendment(s) to this Agreement, and all Resolutions of the Members of the LLC shall constitute the record of the Members of the LLC and of their respective interest therein.

14. <u>Profits and Losses.</u> The profits and losses and all other tax attributes of the LLC shall be allocated to the Initial Member until such time as additional Members are added at which time, the profits and losses and all other tax attributes of the LLC shall be allocated to the Members on the basis of the Members' percentage interests in the LLC.

15. <u>Distributions</u>. Any Distributions of cash or other assets of the LLC (other than in dissolution of the LLC) shall be made in the total amounts and at the times as determined by the Initial Member. Should additional Members be added, distributions of cash or other assets of the LLC (other than in dissolution of the LLC) shall be made in the total amounts and at the times as determined by a majority of the Members. Any such distributions shall be allocated among the Members on the basis of the Members' percentage interests in the LLC.

16. <u>Change in Interests</u>. In the event additional Members are added, and if during any year there is a change in a Member's percentage interest, the Member's share of profits and losses and distributions in that year shall be determined under a method which takes into account the varying interests during the year.

ARTICLE V
VOTING; CONSENT TO ACTION

17. <u>Voting by Members</u>. Until such time as additional Members are added, all decisions will be made by the Initial Member. Should additional Members be added, each Member shall be entitled to vote on any matter voted on by the Members. Voting shall be based on the percentage interest owned by each Member. The action may be taken with or without a meeting.

18. <u>Majority Defined</u>. As used throughout this agreement the term "majority" of the Members shall mean a majority of the ownership interest of the LLC as determined by the records of the LLC on the date of the action. For example, if one Member with a 51% interest votes for passage, and five Members with a combined 49% interest vote against passage, the majority has voted for passage because 51% of the ownership interest has voted for passage.
 Similarly, a reference to a percentage of the Members, for example: "75% of the Members," shall mean a percentage of the ownership interest of the LLC.

19. <u>Majority Required</u>. Should additional Members be added, any action that requires the vote or consent of the Members may be taken upon a majority vote of the Members, based on the Members' percentage interests unless unanimous consent is required by this Agreement.

20. <u>Meetings - Written Consent</u>. Action of the Members or Officers may be accomplished with or without a meeting. If a meeting is held, evidence of the action shall be by Minutes or Resolution reflecting the action of the Meeting, signed by a majority of the Members, or the President and Secretary. Action without a meeting may be evidenced by a written consent signed by a majority of the Members.

21. <u>Meetings</u>. Meetings of the Members shall be held as determined by the Members or as may be called by a majority of the Members, or if a Manager was selected, then by the Manager of the LLC, or if Officers were elected or appointed, by any officer.

22. <u>Termination of Membership.</u> A Member's interest in the LLC shall cease upon the occurrence of one or more of the following events:

(a) A Member withdraws by giving the LLC thirty (30) days written in advance of the withdrawal date. Withdrawal by a Member is not a breach of this Agreement.

(b) A Member assigns all of his/her interest (and not merely a partial interest) to a qualified third party.

(c) A Member dies.

(d) There is an entry of an order by a court of competent jurisdiction adjudicating the Member incompetent to manage his/her person or his/her estate.

(e) In the case of an estate that is a Member, the distribution by the fiduciary of the estate's entire interest in the LLC.

(f) In the case of an entity that is a Member, the distribution upon dissolution of the entity's entire interest in the LLC.

(g) A Member, without the consent of a majority of the Members: (1) makes an assignment for the benefit of creditors; (2) files a voluntary petition in bankruptcy; (3) is adjudicated a bankrupt or insolvent; (4) files a petition or answer seeking for himself any reorganization, arrangement, composition, readjustment, liquidation, dissolution, or similar relief under any statute, law or regulation; (5) files an answer or other pleading admitting or failing to contest the material allegations of a petition filed against him in any proceeding of the nature described in this paragraph; (6) seeks, consents to, or acquiesces in the appointment of a trustee, receiver, or liquidator of the Member or of all or any substantial part of his properties; or (7) if any creditor permitted by law to do so should commence foreclosure or take any other action to seize or sell any Member's interest in the LLC.

(h) If within one hundred twenty (120) days after the commencement of any action against a Member seeking reorganization, arrangement, composition, readjustment, liquidation, dissolution, or similar relief under any statute, law, or regulation, the action has not been dismissed and/or has not been consented to by a majority of the Members.

(i) If within ninety (90) days after the appointment, without a Member's consent or acquiescence, of a trustee, receiver, or liquidator of the Member or of all or any substantial part of the Member's properties, said appointment is not vacated or within ninety (90) days after the expiration of any stay, the appointment is not vacated and/or has not been consented to by a majority of the Members.

(j) Any of the events provided in applicable provisions of state or federal law that are not inconsistent with the dissociation events identified above.

23. Effect of Dissociation. Any dissociated Member shall not be entitled to receive the fair value of his LLC interest solely by virtue of his dissociation. A dissociated Member that still owns an interest in the LLC shall be entitled to continue to receive such profits and losses, to receive such distribution or distributions, and to receive such allocations of income, gain, loss, deduction, credit or similar items to which he would have been entitled if still a Member. For all other purposes, a dissociated Member shall no longer be considered a Member and shall have no rights of a Member.

ARTICLE VII
RESTRICTIONS ON TRANSFERABILITY OF LLC INTEREST; SET PRICE FOR LLC INTEREST

24. LLC Interest. The LLC interest is personal property. A Member has no interest in property owned by the LLC.

25. Encumbrance. A Member can encumber his LLC interest by a security interest or other form of collateral only with the consent of a majority of the other Members. Such consent shall only be given if the proceeds of the encumbrance are contributed to the LLC to respond to a cash call of the LLC.

26. Sale of Interest. A Member can sell his LLC interest only as follows:

(a) If a Member desires to sell his/her interest, in whole or in part, he/she shall give written notice to the LLC of his desire to sell all or part of his/her interest and must first offer the interest to the LLC. The LLC shall have the option to buy the offered interest at the then existing Set Price as provided in this Agreement. The LLC shall have thirty (30) days from the receipt of the assigning Member's notice to give the assigning Member written notice of its intention to buy all, some, or none of the offered interest. The decision to buy shall be made by a majority of the other Members. Closing on the sale shall occur within sixty (60) days from the date that the LLC gives written notice of its intention to buy. The purchase price shall be paid in cash at closing unless the total purchase price is in excess of $25,000.00 in which event the purchase price shall be paid in four (4) equal quarterly installments beginning with the date of closing. The installment amounts shall be computed by applying the following interest factor to the principal amount: interest compounded quarterly at the Quarterly Federal Short-Term Rate existing at closing under the Applicable Federal Rates used for purposes of Internal Revenue Code § 1274(d), or any successor provision.

(b) To the extent the LLC does not buy the offered interest of the selling Member, the other Members shall have the option to buy the offered interest at the Set Price on a pro rata basis based on the Members' percentage interests at that time. If Member does not desire to buy up to his/her proportional part, the other Members can buy the remaining interest on the same pro rata basis. Members shall have fifteen (15) days from the date the LLC gives its written notice to the selling Member to give the selling Member notice in writing of their intention to buy all, some, or none of the offered interest. Closing on the sales shall occur within sixty (60) days from the date that the Members give written notice of their intention to buy. The purchase price from each purchasing Member shall be paid in cash at closing.

(c) To the extent the LLC or the Members do not buy the offered interest, the selling Member can then assign the interest to a non-Member. The selling Member must close on the assignment within ninety (90) days of the date that he gave notice to the LLC. If he does not close by that time, he must again give the notice and options to the LLC and the LLC Members before he sells the interest.

(d) A non-Member purchaser of a Member's interest cannot exercise any rights of a Member unless a majority of the non-selling Members consent to him becoming a Member. The non-Member purchaser will be entitled, however, to share in such profits and losses, to receive such distributions, and to receive such allocation of income, gain, loss, deduction, credit or similar items to which the selling Member would be entitled, to the extent of the interest assigned, and will be subject to calls for contributions under the terms of this Agreement. The purchaser, by purchasing the selling Member's interest, agrees to be subject to all the terms of this Agreement as if he were a Member.

27. <u>Set Price</u>. The Set Price for purposes of this Agreement shall be the price fixed by consent of a majority of the Members. The Set Price shall be memorialized and made a part of the LLC records. The initial Set Price for each Member's interest is the amount of the Member's contribution(s) to the LLC, as updated in accordance with the terms hereof. Any future changes in the Set Price by the Members shall be based upon net equity in the assets of the LLC (fair market value of the assets less outstanding indebtedness), considering the most recent appraisal obtained by the LLC for its assets, as may be adjusted by the Members in their discretion. The initial Set Price shall be adjusted upon demand by a Member but not more than once a year unless all Members consent. This basis for determining the Set Price shall remain in effect until changed by consent of a majority of the Members. The Members will consider revising the basis for determining the Set Price at least annually.

ARTICLE VIII
OBLIGATION TO SELL ON A DISSOCIATION
EVENT CONCERNING A MEMBER

28. <u>Dissociation</u>. Except as otherwise provided, upon the occurrence of a dissociation event with respect to a Member, the LLC and the remaining Members shall have the option to purchase the dissociated Member's interest at the Set Price in the same manner as provided herein and as if the dissociated Member had notified the LLC of his desire to sell all of his LLC interest. The date the LLC received the notice as provided herein triggering the options shall be deemed to be the date that the LLC receives actual notice of the dissociation event.

ARTICLE IX
DISSOLUTION

29. <u>Termination of LLC.</u> The LLC will be dissolved and its affairs must be wound up only upon such a decision by the Initial Member, provided no new Members have been added, or upon the written consent of seventy-five percent (75%) of the all Members should additional Members be added.

30. <u>Final Distributions.</u> Upon the winding up of the LLC, the assets must be distributed as follows: (a) to the LLC creditors; (b) to Members in satisfaction of liabilities for distributions; and (c) to Members first for the return of their contributions and secondly respecting their LLC interest, in the proportions in which the Members share in profits and losses.

ARTICLE X
TAX MATTERS

31. <u>Capital Accounts</u>. Capital accounts shall be maintained consistent with Internal Revenue Code § 704 and the regulations thereunder.

32. <u>Sole Proprietorship/Partnership Election</u>. The Initial Member elects that the LLC be taxed as an S-corporation and shall file the appropriate forms with the Internal Revenue Service to make such election.

ARTICLE XI
RECORDS AND INFORMATION

33. <u>Records and Inspection</u>. The LLC shall maintain at its place of business the Articles of Organization, any amendments thereto, this Agreement, and all other LLC records required to be kept by applicable law, and the same shall be subject to inspection and copying at the reasonable request, and the expense, of any Member.

34. <u>Obtaining Additional Information</u>. Subject to reasonable standards, each Member may obtain from the LLC from time to time upon reasonable demand for any purpose reasonably related to the Member's interest as a Member in the LLC: (1) information regarding the state of the business and financial condition of the LLC; (2) promptly after becoming available, a copy of the LLC's federal, state, and local income tax returns for each year; and (3) other information regarding the affairs of the LLC as is just and reasonable.

ARTICLE XII
MISCELLANEOUS PROVISIONS

35. <u>Amendment</u>. Except as otherwise provided in this Agreement, any amendment to this Agreement may be proposed by a Member. Unless waived by the Members, the proposing Member shall submit to the Members any such proposed amendment together with an opinion of counsel as to the legality of such amendment and the recommendation of the Member as to its adoption. A proposed amendment shall become effective at such time as it has been approved in writing by a majority of the Members. This Agreement may not be amended nor may any rights hereunder be waived except by an instrument in writing signed by the party sought to be charged with such amendment or waiver, except as otherwise provided in this Agreement.

36. <u>Applicable Law</u>. To the extent permitted by law, this Agreement shall be construed in accordance with and governed by the laws of the State of Texas.

37. Pronouns, Etc. References to a Member or Manager, including by use of a pronoun, shall be deemed to include masculine, feminine, singular, plural, individuals, partnerships, corporations or other business entities, where applicable.

38. Counterparts. This instrument may be executed in any number of counterparts each of which shall be considered an original.

39. Specific Performance. Each Member agrees with the other Members that the other Members would be irreparably damaged if any of the provisions of this Agreement are not performed in accordance with their specific terms and that monetary damages would not provide an adequate remedy in such event. Accordingly, it is agreed that, in addition to any other remedy to which the non-breaching Members may be entitled, at law or in equity, the non-breaching Members shall be entitled to injunctive relief to prevent breaches of this Agreement and, specifically, to enforce the terms and provisions of this Agreement in any action instituted in any court of the United States or any state thereof having subject matter jurisdiction thereof.

40. Further Action. Each Member, upon the request of the LLC, agrees to perform all further acts and to execute, acknowledge and deliver any documents which may be necessary, appropriate, or desirable to carry out the provisions of this Agreement.

41. Method of Notices. All written notices required or permitted by this Agreement shall be hand delivered or sent by registered or certified mail, postage prepaid, addressed to the LLC at its place of business or to a Member as set forth on the Member's signature page of this Agreement (except that any Member may from time to time give notice changing his address for that purpose), and shall be effective when personally delivered or, if mailed, on the date set forth on the receipt of registered or certified mail.

42. Facsimiles. For purposes of this Agreement, any copy, facsimile, telecommunication or other reliable reproduction of a writing, transmission or signature may be substituted or used in lieu of the original writing, transmission or signature for any and all purposes for which the original writing, transmission or signature could be used, provided that such copy, facsimile telecommunication or other reproduction shall have been confirmed received by the sending Party.

43. Computation of Time. In computing any period of time under this Agreement, the day of the act, event or default from which the designated period of time begins to run shall not be included. The last day of the period so computed shall be included, unless it is a Saturday, Sunday or legal holiday, in which event the period shall run until the end of the next day which is not a Saturday, Sunday or legal holiday.

WHEREFORE, the Initial Member, being the single Member of this LLC, has executed this Agreement on the [DAY] day of [MONTH], [YEAR].

Signed: _____   Print Name: _____

Address: _____